101 FASCINATING Basketball FACTS

101 Fascinating Facts Series

101 Fascinating Hockey Facts

101 Fascinating Canadian Music Facts

101 Fascinating Canadian Film & TV Facts

101 Fascinating Golf Facts

101 Fascinating Basketball Facts

DALTON HIGGINS

101 FASCINATING Basketball FACTS

DUNDURN PRESS

Publisher: Meghan Macdonald | Acquiring editor: Kwame Scott Fraser | Editor: Allister Thompson
Cover designer: Karen Alexiou
Cover image: basketball and net: Eduard Radu/shutterstock.com; background texture: davidzydd/freepik.com

Library and Archives Canada Cataloguing in Publication

Title: 101 fascinating basketball facts / Dalton Higgins.
Other titles: One hundred one fascinating basketball facts
Names: Higgins, Dalton, author
Identifiers: Canadiana (print) 20250201097 | Canadiana (ebook) 20250201100 | ISBN 9781459755253 (softcover) | ISBN 9781459755260 (EPUB) | ISBN 9781459755277 (PDF)
Subjects: LCSH: Basketball—Miscellanea. | LCSH: Basketball—Anecdotes. | LCGFT: Trivia and miscellanea. | LCGFT: Anecdotes.
Classification: LCC GV885.13 .H54 2025 | DDC 796.32302—dc23

We acknowledge the support of the Canada Council for the Arts and the Ontario Arts Council for our publishing program. We also acknowledge the financial support of the Government of Ontario, through the Ontario Book Publishing Tax Credit and Ontario Creates, and the Government of Canada.

Printed and bound in Canada.

Dundurn Press
1382 Queen Street East
Toronto, Ontario, Canada M4L 1C9
dundurn.com, @dundurnpress

To my in-house crew who are the ultimate engine:
Karen (a.k.a. wifey, a.k.a. my backbone and *front bone)*
Shiloh, Solomon (a.k.a. the kiddos —
the world is yours, like Nas)
Pearlita, Josiah, Milton (a.k.a. The
Higgins Foundation) #NotLikeUs

INTRODUCTION

Basketball. The beautiful game. The best unscripted drama outside of reality TV. From the world of high school basketball, where large numbers of student-athletes look to live out their hoop dreams, to the college NCAA March Madness tournament, where tiny, obscure low- to mid-major conference schools routinely upset blue-blood Power 5 conference powerhouses, all the way over to the NBA, where the most elite global basketball players ply their craft for multi-million-dollar salaries, wherever and however you digest or participate in the sport of basketball, one thing is clear: there is just no other sport quite like it.

Standing at 5'11", I recognized very early in my own basketball journey that despite having played guard for a powerhouse multi-championship-winning high school basketball program, my ceiling in the sport would be quite low, literally and figuratively. As one of the few major sports professions that rewards height — the average height of a male NBA basketball player is 6'7", ten inches taller than the average male height — it is not uncommon to see mutant-like basketball figures gracefully run up and down standard ninety-four-foot courts and side to side with mesmerizing agility as if they were a foot shorter, dribbling, passing, shooting, and dunking with pinpoint precision.

It's also an open secret that kids who win the genetic lottery and grow up to be very tall are strongly encouraged from a young age to take up the sport, regardless of any preordained athletic ability or mobility. Case in point: Toronto-born-and-bred Zach Edey, the two-time back-to-back NCAA national college player of the year (2023, 2024) played baseball and ice hockey for most of his childhood and youth and only took up the sport of basketball in grade 10 because he grew to 7'2" (he is now 7'4") and was strongly encouraged to do so by local basketball coaches and experts.

One of the greatest NBA players of all time, centre Wilt Chamberlain, put that height advantage theory to the test in the late 1950s and throughout the 1960s. Try to envision a single player scoring a hundred points in the game of basketball, where the average *team* nowadays scores just north of a hundred points per game. Well, that's exactly what happened in 1962 when, while playing for the Philadelphia Warriors (pre-Sixers era), Chamberlain completely dominated his New York Knicks opponents on his way to scoring a hundred points. Chamberlain was certainly one of the most skilled big men the game had ever seen, but we also know that standing at 7'1" had a little something to do with that, since the average basketball player's height in the 1960s was 6'5".

Some players who abandon their hoop dreams, either after high school or college, typically try to take up basketball-culture-adjacent jobs, and that's what I did as a journalist, beginning as a college cub reporter covering everything from my own university's basketball team to NCAA college games, then reporting on NBA games and the ultimate gig: covering NBA All-Star Games. While interviewing high-profile high school, college, and pro players, coaches, and agents is a thrill, in between all of that there are virtually an infinite number of intriguing yet obscure facts, personalities, subtleties, and nuances of the sport that often go unreported, underreported, or that remain on the journalists' and content creators' cutting room floor. This book provides the perfect excuse for me to bring some of these beguiling facts to life, to be read and digested by anyone from the casual basketball observer and non-fan all the way to the hardcore roundball junkie.

1

GLO-BALL PHENOMENON

Invented by Canadian doctor and phys. ed. instructor James Naismith in Springfield, Massachusetts, over 130 years ago, no one could have predicted that this beautiful game would go on to capture the imagination, minds, hearts, and souls of the broadest swath of humanity imaginable, across seven continents, and be enjoyed so thoroughly across race, gender, faith, generational, geographical, and class lines. For example, despite the age-old dominance of American male players in the world's most competitive American league (NBA), the last seven league MVP awards have gone to players born outside the U.S.: Shai Gilgeous-Alexander (Canada), three-time winner Nikola Jokić (Serbia), two-time winner Giannis Antetokounmpo (Greece), and Joel Embiid (Cameroon).

What exactly is it about this particular sport that is centred around a bouncy orange circular object and its adjacent hoop that the ball is intended to be tossed inside that commands the strict attention of male/female, Black, white, South Asian, Asian, Indigenous, Latinx, queer, disabled, and most other constituencies in between?

The sport's universal popularity can be attributed to many factors, and certainly one major part of its lure is its accessibility. At a time when the gap between the haves and have nots is widening around the world, the economic equation and resources needed to participate in the sport have largely remained the same over the 130 years since its invention. Equipment-wise, on a basic level, all you need is a pair of sneakers and a basketball to take part, compared with other high-profile major sports like tennis, football, golf, and ice hockey that require costly investments in travel, training, club memberships, and equipment.

For example, suiting up to play ice hockey, even at the lowest amateur and recreational level, still requires you to purchase up to twelve to fourteen pieces of equipment, including a helmet, shoulder pads, gloves, elbow pads, hockey pants, jock strap, skates, hockey stick, shin guards, specialized socks to cover the shin guards, and it goes on and on. And you have to play the sport on a specialized surface (ice), which involves more hard costs tied to renting out a hockey rink.

In that regard, even basketball's playing surface and settings offer up a more firm model of inclusivity, since the game can be played at all skill levels and ages inside a local gym, as its inventor Dr. Naismith envisioned it, or on outdoor courts that can be found anywhere in many urban and rural environments.

Drive through the state of Indiana in the U.S. and you will notice that there is a higher density of hoops per capita than in most regions, since there are basketball hoops everywhere, in people's backyards and front yards, and on open, desolate strips of land. Indiana residents are, in general terms, so proud of their state and its attachment in popular culture to the sport of basketball that they are often referred to as "Hoosiers," a playful nod to their beloved state and Indiana University team's name, identity, and on-court success over the years. In 1986, the fictional Hollywood film *Hoosiers*, starring Gene Hackman, Dennis Hopper, and Barbara Hershey, was a blockbuster success. Its storyline was centred around the state of Indiana's obsession with the sport through the journey of a high school basketball team.

2

RUN, JUMP, SHOOT, THINK

Outside of basketball's innate and organic accessibility framework, there are a plethora of other really good reasons why so many now lay claim to the sport: its continuous fast-paced back and forth flow, its deft combination of athleticism, strategy, and skill that involves mastering some of the key core tenets of the game like dribbling, passing, shooting, rebounding, and blocking shots. And then, within all of that, when you peel back the layers of this beautiful game and do an even more robust Jacques Cousteau–style deep dive into the game's past and present, fully exploring its players, coaches, referees, and fans, from the storied to the obscure, what you'll unearth or find makes the sport all the more intriguing. By mere virtue of the game's depth, speed, grace, flow, science, and global appeal, you know that there would have to be a seemingly bottomless treasure trove of wildly interesting factoids tied to the game.

And that's what I have proudly and painstakingly tried to bring you in this book.

3

WUTHERING (AND INFLATABLE) HEIGHTS

Basketball prospects regularly inflate their height in high school or college to appear taller for recruiting and scouting purposes.

For much of the history of the NBA, by the time most players entered the league, they were typically anywhere between one to three inches shorter than they were listed in the official player's roster guides. LeBron James's son Bronny and NBA Hall of Famer Charles Barkley are both great examples of the discrepancies that exist between an actual player's height and the height that has been recorded on official basketball roster programs. For Barkley's entire twenty-five-year career, he was listed as and thought to be 6'6" (198 cm), whereas the reality of the situation, as he himself admitted, is that he's actually closer to 6'4". "I've been measured at 6'5", 6'4" ¾. But I started in college at 6'6"," he once said.

Likewise, throughout all of Bronny James's senior high school years and in his one year of college at USC (University of Southern California), he was listed as 6'4". After conducting workouts with NBA teams during the NBA Draft process, it was revealed that James was really closer to 6'1". One could also safely assume that many of the players listed at approximately six feet tall are likely shorter than that and are anywhere between 5'9" and 5'11".

Take former Dallas Mavericks guard JJ Barea, for example. He was listed as six feet tall throughout his fourteen-year NBA career, but even his own former teammate, Hall of Famer Dirk Nowitzki, trolled him on social media when he heard that the NBA was cracking down on height inflation.

There is also another variable that adds inches in height to players, and that is the wearing of basketball performance shoes that carry thicker soles. The NBA has always measured players' heights with their shoes on, so what happens when a player chooses to play in shoes that have considerably thicker soles? To keep things in check, that flawed measurement system was altered in the 2019–20 season so that the heights of NBA players are recorded by measuring players with their shoes off.

The flip side to all of this is the cases of NBA players trying to appear shorter for political reasons tied to on-court positioning. For example, two-time NBA champion Kevin Durant, who for years was listed at 6'9" by his teams, is actually closer to seven feet tall without shoes, and that's been an open secret even he admits to. His rationale for being listed shorter than his real height is that coaches can play him in different positions, from point guard and shooting guard to small forward, despite his actual height being closer to that of a traditional "big" power forward or centre. As of 2019 onward, there has been no reason to whip out the measuring tape when players' heights are listed, because those shoes are coming off when it's measurement time.

4

WHITE MEN *CAN* JUMP NOW, APPARENTLY

There is an age-old stereotype, rooted in race, which has posited that white men can't jump. The stereotype comes from the perception that white basketball players are generally less athletic, particularly in terms of vertical leap and dunking ability, compared with their Black counterparts. This stereotype is also rooted in long-running racist stereotypes. Black athletes have often been perceived as more naturally physically gifted in sports that require speed, agility, and jumping ability. This perception has contributed to the stereotype that white athletes lack these same physical attributes.

The 1992 film *White Men Can't Jump*, starring Woody Harrelson and Wesley Snipes, helped popularize the stereotype. It's a just under two-hour comedy that centres around two street basketball hustlers, one white (Harrelson), the other Black (Snipes), and it plays on the notion that white men are not as athletically gifted or as good at playing basketball in general.

It appears that someone forgot to send that memo to one of the whitest of white guys, dunk phenom Mac McClung. Did McClung become the white saviour of the NBA All-Star dunk contest after winning three consecutive championships from 2023 to 2025, all of which happened during Black History Month? No one's sure. But McClung did build on the template set forth by that tiny yet motley cast of white guys in professional basketball who could jump out of the gym before him. Guys like former NBA shooting guard Brent Barry, who won the NBA's 1996 Slam Dunk Contest, two-time NBA All-Star Tom Chambers, who, while standing 6'10" tall was known for his high-flying dunks, or former NBA pro Rex Chapman, who entered the 1990 Slam Dunk Contest and was known to finish fast breaks with athletic dunks dating back to his college career days playing for the University of Kentucky Wildcats. Houston Rockets guard and fellow former Wildcat Reed Sheppard also did much to shift these perceptions when he performed a maximum vertical leap of forty-two inches, landing in a tie with Devin Carter, Keshad Johnson, and Trentyn Flowers for the highest jump at the 2024 NBA Draft Combine. McClung has done more than any white male hooper to help rid society of these ubiquitous unathletic white guy stereotypes, dating back to his days at Gate City High School in Virginia, where he became an Instagram mixtape highlight reel superstar, performing a laundry list of blistering acrobatic in-game dunks.

While he has continued his dunking exploits at all levels, from his college playing days at Georgetown University and Texas Tech all the way to his play in the NBA's G League as an undrafted guard, he hasn't been able to muster enough consideration to play significant minutes in NBA games.

5

DOES SIZE (OF BASKETBALLS) MATTER?

Whether you are talking about participating in kids' recreational or competitive basketball, all the way up to the highest levels of pro women's and men's basketball, there is no one-size-fits-all approach to the different sizes of basketballs being used.

The sizes of basketballs differ to accommodate different age groups, skill levels, and genders, ensuring that the game is appropriately challenging and enjoyable for all players across the spectrum of humanity.

Some of the most marked differences appear across age groups and gender. Between the years of kindergarten to grade 6 you typically use a size 5 basketball, for middle school (grades 7 and 8) you use a size 6 basketball, and for high school (grades 9 to 12) and onwards players use a size 7 basketball. Women's basketball teams use a size 6 basketball, which weighs twenty ounces, is 28.5 inches in circumference, and is slightly smaller and lighter than the size 7 men's basketball, which weighs twenty-two ounces and is 29.5 inches in circumference.

The main reasons for these differences across age groups, gender, and skill level are tied to a number of considerations. Younger players typically use smaller basketballs to match their physical abilities and so that they can develop proper shooting and ball-handling skills. In general terms, the difference between the size of basketballs used across genders (e.g., the women's basketball is slightly smaller and lighter than the men's) is put in place so that the basketball can better fit the average hand size and strength of female players. While there have been discussions within basketball communities about having one standardized basketball that all genders and ages can use, that argument has failed based on the aforementioned considerations tied to the average physical differences between genders and across age groups.

All things considered, when the 2025 NBA All-Star Game's Three-Point Challenge pitted arguably the greatest three-point shooter of all-time, Steph Curry, against the player who might have been considered his female equivalent at the time, the WNBA's Sabrina Ionescu, despite the battle of the sexes theme playing out, which sometimes might mean both parties using the same sporting tools to compete,

Ionescu did shoot with the smaller WNBA basketball that she's accustomed to and only lost by three points to Curry, with a final score of 29–26.

6

CITY OF (HOOP) DREAMS

In basketball lore, New York, the largest city in the United States of America, gets a lot of credit for producing a significant number of elite NBA players (Kareem Abdul-Jabbar, Julius "Dr. J" Erving, Michael Jordan), point guards in particular (Kenny Anderson, Stephon Marbury, Mark Jackson), streetball legends (Earl "the GOAT" Manigault, Richard "Pee Wee" Kirkland), and for nurturing basketball culture in general.

New York is one of only three states, along with California and Texas, in the NBA with more than one basketball franchise. New Yorkers tend to be loyal to their historic New York Knicks franchise, and the Brooklyn Nets, who have only been around since 2012 after being transplanted from New Jersey as the New Jersey Nets, have only once flirted with the potential for great on-court success when they boasted their own "big three" in 2021, a trio of some of the NBA's top players, Kyrie Irving, Kevin Durant, and James Harden. But that experiment failed miserably as the trio only managed to play a total of sixteen games combined, including the regular season and the playoffs, due to a mix of injuries, ego, and poor coaching and management decisions. And outside of splashy NBA sightlines, are you really living if you haven't witnessed a streetball game at Rucker Park, Dyckman Park, or the Cage (West 4th Street) outdoor courts?

Outside of New York, the cities of Chicago, Los Angeles, and Philadelphia consistently produce large numbers of NBA pros due to their histories, resources, basketball infrastructure, and sheer competitiveness. But when it comes to producing Naismith Memorial Basketball Hall of Famers, New York City sits at the top of the heap. The city's strong basketball culture and history of producing top talent have made it the largest contributor to the Hall of Fame roster with twenty-three members, including Kareem Abdul-Jabbar, Julius "Dr. J" Erving, Bernard King, Walt "Clyde" Frazier, and Carmelo Anthony, the most of any city, and New York State also boasts the most Hall of Famers with fifty-six members, the most of any state. In women's basketball, Pennsylvania has the most members in the Hall of Fame with six, including Cynthia Cooper-Dyke and two-sport (tennis, basketball) titan Ora Washington.

7

BASKETBALL WAS PEACHY KEEN (LITERALLY)

Basketball hoops are rigid, sturdy, and functional objects that contain the perfect blend of carbon steel (rim), nylon (net), and glass, polycarbonate, or fibreglass (backboard). But it wasn't always this way. In fact, the first basketball hoops were actually plain old peach baskets — the same ones used to harvest the fruit.

When Dr. James Naismith invented basketball in 1891, he nailed a peach basket to the balcony of the gymnasium at the International YMCA Training School in Springfield, Massachusetts. The bottoms of the baskets were intact, meaning that you had to retrieve the ball after each successful shot.

Eventually, the bottoms of the baskets were removed to allow the ball to pass through freely, and then a series of technological advancements occurred in the early 1900s to replace the peach baskets with standard-issue backboards and metal hoops. In 1906, the metal hoops still remained closed at the bottom, so the players would still have to bring a ladder to the court and manually retrieve the ball after every bucket was scored. Soon, the more modern hoop came to be, with an open-bottomed net, allowing the ball to fall out of the bottom of the hoop. In the early 1900s, glass backboards were introduced and legalized so that spectators on all sides of the court could have better sightlines to view all on-court plays. The Indiana Hoosiers were one of the first college teams to use glass backboards in 1917.

Breakaway rims, invented by Arthur Ehrat in 1976, were introduced to reduce the wear and tear on player's hands after they attempted a dunk and to minimize the potential for backboards to break after a hard dunk was completed. Adjustable hoops came into play in 1986, invented and patented by Lifetime Products, so that the height of a basketball hoop could be raised or lowered based on one's individual needs.

8

ALL CHOKED UP

Basketball coaches, much like bosses at the workplace and teachers in school, can be despised, reviled, and downright hated for committing transgressions, just like any person thrust into a position of authority.

But despite that, there's an unspoken societal rule that morally and legally protects them from being physically harmed by their underlings in the hierarchy of life. Former NBA player Latrell Sprewell must have missed this memo on December 1, 1997, as he went ahead and crossed that boundary by choking his coach on the Golden State Warriors, PJ Carlesimo, throwing a punch at him, and threatening him during a practice session. Naturally, the incident resulted in a groundbreaking sixty-eight-game suspension without pay, one of the longest in NBA history.

The rare and shocking nature of the attack left a lasting impression on the NBA and is thought to have contributed to the NBA handing out more severe fines and punishment than most other professional sports leagues for flagrant acts of physicality dished out by players amongst themselves.

While ugly public disputes between players and coaches are certainly not uncommon (like point god Allen Iverson going on a famous "Practice?" rant in 2002 in response to Sixers coach Larry Brown questioning his attitude toward missing practice and Sacramento Kings centre DeMarcus Cousins's repeated public confrontations with coach George Karl during the 2014–15 season), they very rarely segue into documented physical confrontations.

9
WORLD'S OLDEST BASKETBALL COURT

When most people think about basketball hotspots, they almost always organically and intrinsically conjure up images of historically significant basketball courts in destinations like New York City, known for iconic courts in Harlem (Rucker Park) or Greenwich Village (the Cage), which makes sense given their rich histories of incubating and hosting a virtual who's who of elite-level talent, from Kobe Bryant, Kevin Durant, Kareem Abdul-Jabbar, Earl "the Pearl" Monroe, and Julius "Dr. J" Erving, all the way to Nate Archibald and Wilt Chamberlain.

Likewise, the time-honoured basketball courts at L.A.'s Venice Beach are world famous for their highly competitive games and scenic beachside location. Chicago and Philadelphia are two other large American cities known for their storied streetball hardcourt traditions that have been widely documented. But located in the small, obscure city of St. Stephen, on the east coast of Canada, lies arguably the most historically intriguing basketball playing surface: the world's oldest surviving court. And "this court holds more than just a record," explains Louise Sumner, of the board of directors of the world's oldest basketball court. "It preserves a legacy steeped in the origins of the game itself. It was here that Lyman Archibald, a protégé of James Naismith, the visionary behind basketball, brought the sport to life. During his tenure at the local YMCA, Archibald introduced St. Stephen to this exhilarating game, forever cementing its place in the history of basketball."

And the story of how the world's first basketball court operated once it was up and running is even more interesting. In the 1890s it was not exactly a common thing to see a functioning basketball court anywhere in North America, much less in New Brunswick. So the basketball court sat on the second floor of a building that housed a busy pharmacy on the ground floor. Naturally, citizens wondered aloud about this court, and it triggered a wave of discussion about what exactly was happening in the building and on the court.

As reported in the *Saint Croix Courier*, March 26, 1896, edition, "The proprietor of the St Stephen drug store was waiting on a customer when the earthquake occurred

Sunday evening. The customer was alarmed for a moment but felt reassured when Mr. Waterson informed him that the disturbance was caused by the YMCA athletes practicing in the gymnasium overhead. He was used to that sort of thing. One man who was in a prayer meeting in town says that the shock caused everybody to want to testify."

Fast-forward to today, the court will be getting some much-needed major renovations. Fundraising efforts have been listed to the tune of eighteen million dollars and include a plan to create a full-blown Canadian National Basketball Experience Museum.

10 COURT BEHAVIOUR

To the naked eye, all regulation basketball courts appear the same. But not all courts are considered equal. In fact, there are some sharp distinctions between high school, college, and NBA courts based on size.

NBA and WNBA courts are both ninety-four by fifty feet in width, and FIBA (Fédération Internationale de Basketball) courts are slightly smaller at 91.9 by 49.2 feet, while college and high school courts have a smaller length at eighty-four feet. There are distinct differences in their respective three-point line distances too. The NBA's line is 23.9 feet from the rim, and the WNBA and FIBA three-point line is a bit closer at 22.175 feet, whereas in college basketball it's even closer at 20.9 feet. In high school, it's only 19.75 feet from the rim. Another notable difference between NBA pro courts and college and/or high school courts is the area in the key, or "the paint." In the NBA and WNBA, the paint area is sixteen feet wide, and in FIBA basketball it's 16.1 feet, while it's only twelve feet in high school and NCAA college basketball, making it a lot less easy for "bigs" (centres, power forwards) to execute low-post moves. In the end, what this all means is that making the jump from high school and college basketball to the pros requires some adjustment.

11

COSTLY FREE THROWS

For most basketball players, taking free throw shots is supposed to be a good thing in that they get to take "free" uncontested shots from fairly close to the basket, and if they go in, they are rewarded with a free point.

The free throw line, which is typically located a mere fifteen feet from (and is parallel to) the backboard, is called the "charity stripe" for a reason. On paper and in theory, these free basket-making opportunities should be applauded by all players. All players with the exception of a notable few. Like 2004 NBA champion, four-time NBA All Star, and four-time NBA defensive player of the year Ben Wallace. The strong, bulky power forward who sported a fantastic culturally connected hairdo (an afro) during his playing days and who remains one of the best undrafted players in the history of the game to come from a small Division II school (Virginia Union) couldn't buy a free throw basket if he tried. Wallace remains the NBA player with the lowest career free throw percentage (1,200 shots minimum), shooting 41.4 percent at the free throw line throughout his sixteen-year NBA career.

The poor free throw efficiency of some players, like former New Jersey Net and Portland Trail Blazer Chris Dudley, became a running joke amongst fans, fellow players, and broadcasters, since he also boasted an awkward free throw shooting form, which led to a terrible career free throw shooting percentage of 45.8.

Certainly, the worst-case scenario occurs when players miss free throws during important moments, like during the 2006 playoffs, when the Dallas Mavericks seemed headed to their first NBA championship against the Miami Heat, but in game 3, while up in the series 2–0, ironically, one of the greatest free throw shooting big men in the history of the NBA, Dirk Nowitzki, missed a key freebie down the stretch in the final seconds of the game. The Heat, led by Dwyane Wade, went on to win the momentum-shifting comeback game and the next three games in succession to win the NBA championship.

Even true NBA legends like Hall of Famer Shaquille O'Neal, who shot hundreds upon hundreds of bricks at the free throw line and who once even missed all eleven of his free throw attempts in a single game, could have a terrible career free throw percentage of 52.7. O'Neal was so bad that the "hack-a-Shaq" basketball strategy was invented that involves intentionally fouling a poor free-throw shooter, typically late in games, to exploit their weakness at the line. This strategy aims to disrupt the opposing team's offence and gain possession of the ball without allowing a high-percentage shot. The term literally originated from the practice of fouling Shaq. So, when it came to shooting free throws, there's no question that O'Neal was bad, but even he wasn't Wallace bad.

12

INDIGENOUS PEOPLE MAKE THEIR MARK

In the modern NBA, the Native American presence has been scant, with few players over the past twenty years claiming Indigenous identity.

In recent times, NBA champion Kyrie Irving, who is 25 percent Native American (his father is Black/African American and his mother is half Black/African American and half Lakota) has paid homage to his Indigenous heritage in interviews, beginning in 2018, and through his footwear (he wore some special Anta Kai 1 "Chief Hélà" Indigenous culture–themed sneakers during the 2024 playoffs). Irving's mother, Elizabeth Larson, is of Sioux heritage from the Standing Rock reservation in South Dakota, and he was given the Lakota name Little Mountain at a ceremony held at the Prairie Knights Pavilion venue.

The only other Indigenous players to play a role in winning an NBA championship are Patty Mills, who is Kokatha (Aboriginal Australian). His father, Benny, is an Indigenous Torres Strait Islander, and his mother, Yvonne, is an Aboriginal Australian, the offspring of an Aboriginal Australian father and white mother. Mills won the 2014 Larry O'Brien Championship Trophy as a member of the San Antonio Spurs team that also featured superstars Kawhi Leonard, Tim Duncan, and Tony Parker. Bison Dele was a member of the 1997 Chicago Bulls championship team that boasted Michael Jordan, and he changed his name during his last season with the Pistons, 1998–99, from Brian Williams, to honour his Cherokee ancestry.

Although not discussed widely, the Indigenous presence in the NBA goes way back to the mid-1950s, not long after the league started in 1949, when 6'10" centre and California native Phil Jordon stepped on the court during the 1956–57 season as a member of the New York Knicks, becoming the first Native American to play in the NBA. Jordon, who played seven productive seasons in the league, averaging 10.9 points and 6.9 rebounds per game before dying at the age of thirty-one, had a white mother, and his father was of the Wailaki and the Nomlaki tribes. In a strange twist of fate, the historic game on March 2, 1962, in which Wilt Chamberlain scored a hundred points was the same game that Jordon fell ill, and he was slated to cover Chamberlain in that game as an opposing centre.

A small number of NBA players with Indigenous backgrounds have played in the league and have also had success at the collegiate level, including 6'11" centre Cherokee Parks, who won a national championship in 1992 as a key member of a tough Duke University squad, and MarJon Beauchamp, was who drafted by the Milwaukee Bucks with the twenty-fourth pick in the NBA Draft lottery. He is a descendant of both the Mission Indians and La Jolla Band of Luiseño Indians from Southern California. Beauchamp founded the MarJon Beauchamp All-Native Tournament in 2024 to showcase Native American basketball players.

Arguably the largest and most renowned all-Indigenous basketball tournament in the U.S. is produced and hosted by NABI Nation, and there are a flurry of other Indigenous/Native American basketball leagues, including the HOOPS (Honoring Our Original People in Sports) League, which encourages the participation of Indigenous community members in basketball, and the Battle of the Nations, which features dozens of teams from Native American tribes across the country that battle for bragging rights and cash prizes.

13

FOUR-POINTERS, IT'S TIME

Is it now time to formally implement a four-point shot in the NBA and the global professional basketball mix, given that the players have achieved some level of mastery over the other two scoring options, two- and three-pointers? The four-point shot being added to the NBA, the greatest basketball league in the world, might be on the horizon.

Former NBA pro and notorious three-point shooter Antoine Walker, when once asked why he shoots so many three pointers, proclaimed, "Because there are no fours."

And it's not an entirely new concept, since the semi-pro American Basketball Association counts any basket made from beyond half-court as a four-point field goal. It's already been experimented with in the NBA All-Star

Game. And the four-point shot and movement has been progressing slightly under the radar over the last few years, with the Harlem Globetrotters, the hundred-year-old vaudeville-style basketball entertainment showcase, implementing the shot in 2022. The Philippines Basketball Association, which used a four-point line in their all-star games, officially added a four-point line that will be twenty-seven feet (their three-point line sits at the twenty-three-foot mark) to their regular season games in 2024–25.

Likewise, Jeff Kwatinetz and rapper/entrepreneur Ice Cube, cofounders of the Big3 basketball league, have gotten rave reviews steering the ship of the only three-on-three professional basketball league that has pushed the mainstreaming of a four-point field goal. Many think that this outside-the-box implementation of a shot that is more difficult to make but provides more box score scoring numbers and incentives was long overdue. In Big3 games, there are three distinct circles beyond the three-point line that are designated as four-point shot areas. And with this inclusion, the flow of the game has gone swimmingly well.

The WNBA also seem to have a more forward-thinking view on growing the game, since they also implemented a four-point field goal at their 2022 All-Star Game. In this instance, a four-pointer occurs when a player shoots and scores from one of two circles located on each side of the court about twenty-eight feet from the basket. That being said, this feat was relegated to the All-Star Game, so no one's entirely sure whether this shot will get treated as something other than an entertaining novelty shot, comparable to the contests run by many professional basketball franchises that reward arbitrary or handpicked fans who shoot a basketball from half court and hit the shot with a cash prize of thousands of dollars.

Clearly, the idea of a four-point shot in basketball isn't entirely new. What hasn't happened, though, is it getting anywhere near being treated as something less than a sideshow you tack on to niche events with high entertainment value (all-star games). It's not taken seriously enough to be implemented in the more serious day-to-day workings of high school, college, and professional basketball.

Is there a reason the world's most important and popular league, the NBA, hasn't seriously looked at adopting a four-point shot? And if so, what distance would it have to be shot from? Somewhere between the half-court line and the three-point line? Regardless, one thing we do know is that if a four-point shot were implemented, shooting percentages would be really low, and do we really want to watch games where eighty percent of the shots taken are not going in and where airballs become more routine? To get a sneak peak of what happens when players habitually start shooting the rock from beyond the three-point arc, just take a look at NBA All-Star Games over the last decade. The game itself is becoming virtually unwatchable for this same reason.

14
I'M COMING OUT

In the over seventy-five-year history of the NBA, only one player has come out as gay while playing on an NBA contract. And as far as coming-out parties go, in professional sports, basketball has led the way across the four major American pro sports leagues (NFL, NHL, MLB, NBA), so that's not saying much.

It was only in 2013 that Jason Collins, then a thirty-four-year-old free agent, became the first active male athlete to come out as gay in a cover story for *Sports Illustrated*. NBA veteran John Amaechi came out six years prior, in 2007, but that was after his playing days were done, which perhaps felt safer as far as impacting his personal safety and career moves. Interestingly, not one active NBA player has come out since then, so it might have created an unconscious chilling effect.

In the court of public opinion, the NBA, despite its transgressions in areas of ownership and genuine economic inclusion given its majority Black participation rates, is considered to be a more progressive sports league when it comes to its handling of pressing social issues like anti-Black racism versus other major pro sports leagues like the NHL or MLB, perhaps because a disproportionate number of its players have almost always been Black, so the pink elephant in the room had to get dealt with head-on, in theory.

But in the area of sexuality, it's curious that no other player has come out since Collins, given his theoretical kicking down of the door. In the women's game, coming out as gay has not been an issue and is quite routine and normalized, with little pushback. For example, in the WNBA, league champion, two-time league scoring leader, and ten-time All-Star Brittney Griner has come out as queer, as has two-time MVP Elena Delle Donne. In the 2024 WNBA All-Star Game that pitted the women's USA Olympic basketball team against the WNBA All-Stars in Phoenix, Arizona, the openly out couple of DeWanna Bonner and Alyssa Thomas — who also just happened to be teammates on the Connecticut Sun — played against each other.

So, what is it about the men's game that has prevented this from happening? Is it homophobia? Toxic masculinity?

Both? Gallup estimates that more than 7 percent of the U.S. adult population is lesbian, gay, bisexual, or transgender, and that about 3 percent of American men are gay. Of the on-average 450 players in the NBA, statistically speaking, you'd figure that around fourteen players might be gay and in the closet. To avoid any fears of lack of inclusion, gay activists and entrepreneurs have floated the idea of having a gay professional league, and the National Gay Basketball Association (NGBA) has been around since 2006. The NGBA league boasts more than a thousand members, but it is more recreationally centred and anchored around raising awareness and participation rates of gay basketball players than it is of incubating and showcasing elite professional-level players.

15

RIM ROCKING

Men's basketball without dunks is like a burger without the fries — the two go hand in hand. Watching a player like the Memphis Grizzlies' NBA All-Star point guard Ja Morant or USA Olympic team member and Minnesota Timberwolves shooting guard Anthony Edwards throw down a hyperathletic dunk is the ultimate adrenaline pump. But what happens when a high-powered dunk becomes too much to bear for the physical structure of the rim and backboard that has to endure the sheer force?

Although it's not a common occurrence, every so often a player will throw down a nasty dunk that's so hard, it shatters the backboard. And Hall of Fame centre Shaquille O'Neal has been a major culprit in this area, through no fault of his own. Standing at 7'1" and weighing in at an average playing weight of 325 pounds during his career, Shaq was a notorious rim-wrecker by virtue of the power of his dunks, and he's reputed to have destroyed twelve backboards over a nineteen-year playing span. His shoe endorsement company, Reebok, had fun with this unique phenomenon and created a whole promotional campaign where he dunks, breaks a backboard, and then it transforms into a broken rim tree for every rim he has broken.

On the NBA's side of the ledger, due to the carnage caused by Shaq, the league implemented newer, stronger backboards and rims. When basketball backboards shatter, it can cause games to be cancelled or delayed because the backboard needs to be replaced very quickly for the game to continue. For leagues not named the NBA or NCAA, which have bloated revenues and budgets, the typical rim and backboard replacement costs can be daunting. Shattering a backboard can also be quite dangerous because when the backboard shatters, all kinds of small splintered pieces of the glass can fly all over the place, with shards hitting players, spectators, or referees.

Darryl Dawkins, affectionately referred to as Chocolate Thunder, a 6'11" centre/power forward and the first player in the history of the NBA to be drafted straight out of high school, by the Philadelphia 76ers, due to his sheer size, strength, and physicality, was also the first player to break an NBA backboard with a monster dunk in 1979 in a game against the then Kansas City Kings, which led to the league installing breakaway rims and more sturdy shatterproof backboards to deal with physically superior players like him who might leave a string of broken rims in different arenas due to their dunking prowess.

16

SAVING IT FOR LAST

It's an open secret that staying monogamous while being an NBA superstar is a challenging proposition at best. When young basketball players coming out of college become independently wealthy overnight, all kinds of unexpected phenomena come into play. From basketball icon Wilt Chamberlain claiming to have slept with twenty thousand women and former Los Angeles Lakers great Magic Johnson admitting to having stretches of three hundred sexual partners a year, to Andrei Kirilenko's wife, Masha Lopatova, publicly admitting to allowing him one night a year to have sex with other women, or Zion Williamson's sexual trysts with adult film star Moriah Mills while he was expecting a child with his actual girlfriend, the NBA lifestyle is littered with groupies camping out across the thirty NBA franchise cities, perpetually looking to hook up with wealthy, influential players. And many players willingly seek out these types of temporary relationships and one-night stands, so it's a two-way street.

And then on the complete opposite end of that spectrum there's AC Green. Despite debauchery and fornication being almost a formal part of professional basketball life, Green, who won three NBA titles with the Los Angeles Lakers and set a record for playing in 1,192 consecutive games, was having none of that. In fact, Green, a born-again Christian, took a vow of celibacy during his playing days and proudly remained a virgin for his entire sixteen-year career. In a segment for ESPN's *30 for 30* series of documentary shorts, "A.C. Green: Iron Virgin," his former teammates tell tales of how they would invite him out to party with women or send women to his hotel room, but they couldn't break his unwavering commitment to abstinence. Or, when being wooed and tempted by teammates with offers of women, Green would wave his bible around and say things like, "No, I won't go out with you guys, but I'll pray for you guys,'" says his ex-Lakers teammate Michael Cooper.

During his entire teenage and young adult life, Green was the textbook definition of chaste; while attending Oregon State University, he reportedly saw a copy of *Playboy* magazine in the school's bookstore and then organized a protest on campus to express his displeasure. Green did eventually lose his virginity to his wife, Veronique, when he got married in 2002. And the secular crowd might consider that a very happy ending.

17

NO LOGO, YES LOGO

It would make sense that the most famous and widely circulated basketball-player-centred logo belongs to Michael Jordan, arguably the greatest basketball player of all time, with his Jumpman logo, which Nike created in 1988 to help promote their Air Jordan line of sneakers and sporting apparel.

The logo is a silhouette of a photo featuring Jordan executing a one-handed dunk with his legs spread out. The world's bestselling rapper, Drake, even recorded a hit song alongside rapper Future titled "Jumpman" that directly references the logo in its song title while commemorating its significance in the lyrics. Given that Jordan Brand sponsors a wide range of college and professional sports teams, the Jumpman logo can be seen on the uniforms of everyone from his alma mater, the University of North Carolina's basketball and football teams, all the way to the legendary French football team Paris Saint-Germain's UEFA Champions League uniforms.

But arguably the most time-honoured basketball logo that can never fall victim to trends is the NBA logo, which is actually a silhouette of Jerry West, the late Los Angeles Lakers legend. At first glance, the logo appears like an anonymous, generic basketball player dribbling a ball. But it's Jerry West, and the NBA reportedly never really came out and said that it was him, for reasons that are still unknown, though it's been suggested that perhaps the league would have been on the hook for a licensing fee to West if it was spelled out to him that the logo featured his likeness.

The logo was designed in 1969 by highly regarded graphic designer Alan Siegel, who wanted to create a timeless and recognizable emblem for the league. Siegel used a photograph of West in action, captured by sports photographer Wen Roberts, as the basis for the silhouette. West, a Lakers legend, was chosen not only for his playing style and aesthetics in the photograph but also for his status as one of the game's greats. Despite the NBA never officially acknowledging West as the model for the logo, it has become widely accepted and recognized as his silhouette. West himself expressed mixed feelings about being the logo, appreciating the honour but also feeling that other great players might deserve it just as much.

18

MARCH MAN-NESS

Every year during the month of March, basketball enthusiasts worldwide tune into the NCAA men's basketball tournament, where sixty-eight teams battle it out for college basketball supremacy in a single elimination game format.

Appropriately titled "March Madness," the madness part of the equation comes into play because top ranked teams from the Power 5 conferences are routinely upset in the tournament by more obscure teams from smaller conferences, and the games often end up being absolute nail-biters with the final outcomes determined by last-second shots. March Madness games are not for the faint of heart. The NCAA women's basketball tournament just happens to occur during March too and carries similar drama-filled storylines pitting smaller David teams versus Goliaths, and the outcomes can sometimes feel just as unpredictable.

That being said, the term "March Madness" has historically and singularly been associated with the NCAA men's basketball tournament, which dates back to 1939. It gained widespread popularity in the 1980s and became a trademark of the NCAA. However, the term was not officially used for the women's tournament until 2021, and no one is exactly sure why. Before that time, there wasn't a specific reason why women's college basketball players weren't allowed to use the term. It's likely that it simply wasn't as commonly associated with the women's tournament due to gender inequity, as well as differences in exposure, coverage, and marketing efforts between the men's and women's games.

In recent years, the NCAA has made a concerted effort to feature the women's tournament more prominently, including the use of the "March Madness" branding, recognizing the achievements and talents of women's college basketball players. And they would be fools not to, considering that some women's NCAA tournament games, like the 2023 Iowa versus Louisiana State University game featuring superstars Caitlin Clark and Angel Reese, had a larger viewership than any of the men's games. At 12.3 million viewers, the game even had more viewers than the 2023 NBA Finals and the 2023 World Series.

19

ORANGE IS THE NEW BLACK

By and large, regardless of what country or league you play basketball in, from recreational to college to pro, most basketballs are orange in colour. But it wasn't always this way. Basketballs actually used to be brown before the late 1950s. And it was during that time that the head coach of the NCAA men's basketball program at Butler University, Tony Hinkle, independently thought it was time for a colour switch because he believed that both the players and fans had a hard time tracking the ball on the court as it was shot and passed around. Hinkle believed that orange would work because of its brightness and more obvious visibility, so in 1957 he collaborated with sports equipment company Spalding to develop a new basketball prototype. In the following year, during the 1958 NCAA Finals in Louisville Kentucky, the new and improved orange basketball made its debut and was a runaway success. So much so that the orange ball became the standard colour for most basketball organizations.

While multicoloured basketballs have been used throughout the history of the game for different purposes, dating back to the American Basketball Association (1967–76), which used a red, white, and blue ball before its merger with the NBA, league executives believed that the multicoloured ball clashed with the hardwood floor colour on television broadcasts. The Harlem Globetrotters have always preferred to use this same multicoloured red, blue, and white colour scheme to help set them apart from other teams and to enhance the visual appeal of their theatrical performances. Likewise, the WNBA has also used a multicoloured orange-and-white ball since the league's inception in 1997 to differentiate their league from others and create a distinct brand identity that is synonymous with women's pro basketball in the U.S.

20
HOOP DOCTORS

When you hear the words "doctor" and "basketball" in the same sentence, you're certainly not thinking about a baller being an actual medical doctor, though the baller cum doctor thing has happened.

And we're not talking about Julius "Dr. J" Erving, who wasn't a trained doctor, nor was he a recipient of an honorary doctorate. He was called a "doctor" because of his absolute mastery of elite-level basketball skills like dunking. Or perhaps people might be thinking of Darnell "Dr. Dunk" Hillman, who won the NBA's Slam Dunk Contest in 1977. Whatever the case, the fact is there are only four hundred jobs in the NBA per year, and a kid's chance of becoming a doctor is a lot greater. While there are thousands upon thousands of medical doctors in cities, states, towns, and countries, but it's quite rare for basketball players to become trained doctors due to the extensive education and training required. It typically doesn't align with a professional sports career timeline. However, there are some instances where former players have actually pursued medical degrees or careers in related fields after retiring from basketball. One notable example is Tom McMillen, who played in the NBA during the 1970s and later went on to earn a medical degree from Georgetown University. He practised briefly as an orthopedic surgeon before transitioning into a successful career in politics, serving in the U.S. House of Representatives from 1987 to 1993.

21
HOOP DREAMS

Today, there is an entire cottage industry of great basketball films and documentaries. This ranges from the ten-part *The Last Dance*, which took viewers on the epic tell-all journey of Michael Jordan's last championship season with the Chicago Bulls in 1998, to *The Fab Five*, which trailed the lives of the University of Michigan's highly touted freshman starting lineup (Chris Webber, Juwan Howard, Jalen Rose, Ray Jackson, and Jimmy King), both on and off the court. And they all mostly have the 1994 documentary *Hoop Dreams* to thank. Directed by Steve James, the film follows the lives of two Chicago high school students, William Gates and Arthur Agee, over a five-year period as they pursue their dream of becoming professional basketball players. While the film brilliantly captures the ups and downs of the two boys trying to land college scholarships, and the role that race and class play in these navigations, despite its widespread critical acclaim the film was actually snubbed by the Oscars for a Best Documentary Feature nomination in what is considered one of the biggest slights in Academy Awards history.

That misstep was so egregious — many thought the film would win an Oscar, and noted film critic Roger Ebert called it the best film of the entire 1990s, never mind it not even getting nominated — that the Academy was forced to immediately change its voting process for documentaries. They removed their archaic "flashlight system" (where voting members with flashlights could stop a screening due to lack of interest after fifteen minutes) because of this *Hoop Dreams* snafu to avoid further embarrassment and controversy.

Steve James chalked up his film's omission and the accompanying controversy it created to some of the old system's flaws tied to the lack of age diversity of the Academy voting members: "It used to be older members of the Academy, not all documentary makers, and skewed toward retirees because they were the ones who had the time to look at all of the films under consideration."

22

SHOOTERS SHOOT

When Kim Jong Un, the supreme leader of North Korea, is not busy issuing threats to Western democracies, he's usually balling while shot calling.

Basketball is one of the most popular sports in North Korea, and Kim Jong Un is not only a huge fan of the game, but he's also a Chicago Bulls superfan who reportedly owns an extensive Michael Jordan video library that features every single one of his Royal Airness's NBA games. While not much is known about the national team's tryout process, training techniques, playing schedule, salaries, or the future of the sport in the country due to strict government media controls, North Koreans have been known to play their own version of the sport, which carries a distinctive twist. For example, when a player hits a traditional three-point shot and it doesn't hit the rim, or what Westerners refer to as a "swish," they are rewarded with four points. Also, if a player takes a free throw and misses any shots, points are deducted from the scoresheet.

While the NBA and other professional basketball leagues have been in no rush to travel to North Korea to play exhibition or competitive games or help grow the sport there due to the laundry list of human rights violations perpetrated by the government, four-time NBA champion, Hall of Famer, and American bad boy Dennis Rodman is the only NBA player to have visited North Korea. Rodman reportedly formed a peculiar friendship with Jong Un, having visited the country multiple times to assist and train the national basketball team. Rodman, who rightly or wrongly marches to the beat of his own drummer, has also publicly apologized for visiting and creating confusion tied to international relations between his homeland, the United States of America, and North Korea.

23

THE GOAT DEBATE THAT KEEPS ON GIVING

Basketball is the only professional sport in which the idea of an undisputed GOAT (greatest of all time) is debated as fiercely, harshly, and consistently as Michael Jordan versus LeBron James.

It's a war of attrition as LeBron James's superfans (some dubbed LeBronsexuals) have made their presence known both on and offline, questioning the prevailing notion that Michael Jordan is the greatest player ever to play the game. As both sides cling to their own respective basketball demigod with cult-like fervour, concepts like objectivity, neutrality, non-partisanship, and being unbiased all go out the window. Unlike in most other North American pro sports, where there are, in general terms, some unanimous choices for who the GOAT is, including the NHL (Wayne

Gretzky), NFL (Tom Brady), and tennis (Serena Williams), in basketball circles it doesn't even matter how the stats stack up at this point. So we won't bother presenting any "tales of the tape," regular season versus playoff stats, championship wins versus playoff flame-outs, accolades and awards, or any more hard data and statistics on who is the GOAT.

MJ won six championships. LeBron has only won four while jumping around from team to team, blah, blah, yada, yada. Forget the stats. On social media platforms like Instagram and TikTok, there are literally hundreds of devoted sports and fan pages arguing on both LBJ and MJ's behalf, with those numbers expected to double over time. It's such a contentious debate that it has indisputably become the GDOT (greatest debate of all time), never mind who is the GOAT. And in more recent times, stans, superfans, and groupies stumping for either player have become hazardous to one's health. Case in point: back in 2013, an MJ/LeBron debate got so intense that it led to three men being stabbed at the Ba'Runi Hotel & Grille in Pittsburgh. In 2015, at State College, Pennsylvania, this same debate led to an assault charge and a stint in jail for a twenty-two-year-old who was charged with aggravated assault, uttering terroristic threats, and simple assault.

24 O CANADA!

Why is Canada, of all places, producing more NBA players than every other country in the world not named the United States of America? Especially given that Canada has traditionally been known as a hockey-loving country producing scads of puck stars?

Well, this land of beer, hockey, rock n' roll, poutine, and maple syrup has become an absolute hotbed for all kinds of pure basketball talent, and a fair number of unicorns too. If you took a glance at NBA draft boards and regular season rosters over the past ten years, you will have noticed that there's almost always a Canadian player or two landing in the first few rounds of the NBA draft or participating in the NBA playoffs and playing a big role in their team's success. In 2025, the NBA championship finals series featured four

Canadian players: the Indiana Pacers' Andrew Nembhard and Bennedict Mathurin, and the Oklahoma City Thunder's Shai Gilgeous-Alexander and Luguentz Dort. In 2019 alone, six Canadian players (RJ Barrett, Nickeil Alexander-Walker, Brandon Clarke, Mfiondu Kabengele, Marial Shayok, and Ignas Brazdeikis) were drafted. In more recent years, from Golden State Warriors 2022 NBA champion and All-Star Andrew Wiggins and 2023 NBA champion and All-Star Jamal Murray all the way to 2025 NBA champion and MVP Shai Gilgeous-Alexander, who became the first Canadian to win the NBA scoring title, there is clearly something brewing in the north.

In NCAA college basketball ranks, it gets even more interesting, as giant Canadian 7'4" centre Zach Edey won the NCAA Player of the Year award, awarded to the best player in U.S. college basketball, back-to-back in 2023 and 2024 and was drafted with the ninth overall pick in the 2024 NBA Draft by the Memphis Grizzlies.

Canada is a very cold country with winters sometimes lasting six to seven months, so there's nothing in the natural environment that lends itself to being a basketball hotbed, just like how a Black Jewish guy (Drake) bred in an upper-middle-class neighbourhood in Toronto being the world's most successful rapper might make even less sense.

Local basketball coach and expert Roy Rana knows a thing or two about what Canadian basketball success looks like from the grassroots level as a multiple Canadian High School Coach of the Year honouree who coached arguably the greatest Ontario Federation of School Athletic Associations championship–winning Canadian high school team of all time, Eastern Commerce, a squad that featured 6'10" University of Kentucky NCAA champion and NBA All-Star Jamaal Magloire. He also coached high-winning-percentage teams at the university level (Toronto Metropolitan University made six National Championship appearances in nine seasons under his helm) and was head coach of the World Select Team at the Nike Hoop Summit that featured the future 2021, 2022, and 2024 NBA MVP Nikola Jokić and 2023 NBA MVP Joel Embiid, and coached the first U19 Canadian national basketball team, featuring NBA Toronto Raptors guard RJ Barrett, to the country's first ever gold medal at the 2017 FIBA World Championships.

As to why Canada is now producing a disproportionate number of top-tier college and professional basketball players and also boasts the second most players in the NBA of any nation in the world next to the U.S. since 2018, Rana has his own theories.

"Our diversity has become our strength," says Rana, who has had assistant coaching stints in the NBA with the Sacramento Kings and both assistant and head coaching jobs with the German, Jordan, and Egyptian national teams. "Immigration brought the first wave of Canadian basketball icons from the Caribbean, including players like David Joseph (father of NBA veteran Cory Joseph), the Llewellyns (Radcliffe, Bobby), Phil Dixon, Richard Stewart, Bobby Allen, Joe Alexander, who laid a foundation in a time when the game was still trying to find a way to be inclusive. Today's generation is a product of these trailblazers, both literally and figuratively. The new immigrants who came to Canada from Europe, Asia, and Africa have fallen in love with a game that looks like them and also is viewed as cooler in our culture. Hockey stayed a traditional sport, and basketball became an aspirational one.

"The younger generation can watch the Toronto Raptors and in general have access to NBA basketball on multiple media platforms that we did not have in our time. This has further fuelled a passion for the sport, which is more in line with youth culture in modern Canada. Our coaches, mentors, and community delivering the sport at the grassroots level are much more educated and savvy in understanding the process of developing but more importantly in placing elite talent in environments where they can be evaluated amongst the best in their age group globally. The result has been a rapid realization that Canada is a legitimate market for élite basketball players who can play at the highest levels."

25

IT'S YOUR BIRTHDAY. AND YOURS TOO. AND YOU IN THE BACK.

The likelihood of you having the exact same birthday and birthdate as your immediate work colleague is pretty slim. So then how do you explain the 2015 Dallas Mavericks roster that featured three players (Deron Williams, JJ Barea, and Raymond Felton) playing the exact same position (point guard) and who all had the exact same birthdate of June 26, 1984? You simply don't. You chalk it up to some divine intervention. And you do anything but try to make any sense of it all, because it feels like it's literally statistically impossible. That year, as rotating point guards, they all shared minutes, and that same season was also the last year that the Dirk Nowitzki–led Mavericks team would make the playoffs before his retirement. So perhaps this holy multi-birthdate trinity was an omen. Or it was written.

26

SHOOT. SCORE. REPEAT.

When college basketball fans think of high-powered, high-scoring offences, they might naturally be looking at NCAA Division I schools from the Power 5 conferences (Southeastern Conference, Atlantic Coast Conference, Big 10, Big 12, and the Pac-12) that typically dominate both regular season league and March Madness playoff tournament play. And then there's Grinnell College.

This small liberal arts college based in Grinnell, Iowa, which plays in the lower and far less competitive Division III echelon, plays a high-scoring, unorthodox style of basketball that focuses on scoring the maximum amount of points during a regulation forty-minute game, at all costs. And in 2012, Grinnell guard Jack Taylor scored a jaw-dropping 138 points in a 179–104 win over lowly regarded

Faith Baptist Bible College, hitting twenty-seven of his seventy-one three-point shot attempts.

Utilizing the "the Grinnell System," the team does full five-man substitutions, presses their opponents for forty minutes, and encourages players to shoot the ball within the first seven seconds of the shot clock. While their games feel more like video games than basketball games, Coach David Arseneault Jr., who took over the program from his dad and runs the same offence that his dad ran back in 2012 when that scoring feat happened, considers Taylor's scoring record to be a godsend for the school. "Most recruits, the first thing they ask me about is Jack Taylor's 138-point game," Arseneault Jr. said. "The aftereffects are still just so lasting in a positive effect for our program."

27

WHEN BASKETBALL AND *BET UNCUT* BLUR

The goal of all youth high school basketball tournaments is to get bums in seats, to cover basic hard costs, like paying for referees and refreshments, and so that competitors aren't playing to empty stands. And sometimes that means ramping up a tournament's usual tried-and-tested marketing efforts.

But when a Newark, New Jersey, high school launched their NBA Baddies Basketball Tournament and decided to promote it with the tagline "Nuttin Butt Azz," putting bums in seats became the least of their concerns, since there was no shortage of real-life bums to be found on the court in the lead-up to the proposed July 21, 2024, tournament date. The tournament's X-rated marketing efforts came complete with teaser videos that showed scantily clad young women wearing sexually provocative attire, baring near-naked bums, while dribbling basketballs and twerking. It was just too much for the Newark Board of Education staff, who promptly cancelled the tournament. Local party promoter Big Fendi, who produced the promotional clip, apologized for the misstep on Instagram: "Things went a little left and got out of control. I take full responsibility for that because you had no idea what these girls would be wearing."

28
HOOPS & HIP HOP

The worlds of hip-hop and basketball are inextricably linked. Some theories link the two professions to their racialized low-income and low-barrier-to-entry origins. Many basketball players want to rap, and likewise, most rappers wish they could be ballers. Off the court, we see these synergies play out in boardrooms; for example, iconic Grammy Award–winning rapper Jay Z was once Reebok's head of basketball operations and now works as the creative director of Puma Basketball.

Few hybridized rapper/basketball players have been able to simultaneously pull off both professions with any semblance of high integrity or output. Also, very few rappers have done double duty and have been capable of playing basketball at a professional level. J. Cole stands out from the pack because he's had a few stints playing in the Basketball Africa League for the Rwanda Patriots Basketball Club and the Canadian Elite Basketball League with the Scarborough Shooting Stars. Certainly, others, like superstar rapper and entrepreneur Master P's short stint with the Toronto Raptors training camp, made many basketball fans say uhhh — and not in a good way.

On the flip side, a whole slew of basketball players, including icons Kobe Bryant, Dame Lillard, Allen Iverson, and Chris Webber, have all released rap records to little sales or fanfare and have been instructed by concerned social media types and journalists to keep their day jobs. In fact, Shaquille O'Neal has been the only NBA player in history to record rap albums and have them perform sales-wise very well; Shaq recorded one platinum-selling album, his debut, *Shaq Diesel*, signed to Jive Records, and he released four more full-length solo studio albums.

Basketball players often get name-dropped in rap songs, with some players being mentioned more frequently than others. Michael Jordan leads the pack, showing up in songs from a wide range of popular rappers, like Jadakiss ("Why"), Drake ("Over My Dead Body"), Kendrick Lamar ("Michael Jordan," "The Blacker the Berry"), Jay Z ("Encore"), and Lil Wayne ("Believe Me"), while others, like LeBron James, Kobe Bryant, Allen Iverson, and Steph Curry, show up in occasional rap lyrics for reasons that demonstrate how rap lyrics put a mirror to reality and in these cases are used to celebrate a certain player's absolute dominance of the sport.

29
AGE IS ONLY A NUMBER

There was a time when NBA players could skip college altogether and be drafted straight out of high school. For some of the greatest players of all time, like NBA Hall of Famer Moses Malone, the first basketball player to make the leap directly in 1974 at age nineteen from high school to playing in the American Basketball Association (which later merged with the NBA), it made perfect sense. While playing for Petersburg High School in Virginia, Malone was so dominant as a centre that watching him score on and manhandle his opponents was like watching a man playing against boys, and his squad didn't lose a game in back-to-back years.

Former Detroit Piston Reggie Harding was the first high school player to be drafted by an NBA team (Detroit

Pistons, 1962), but he couldn't play in the league until the following year due to league rules at the time, and he had a very brief NBA career, languishing in obscurity.

Then you had NBA legend Kobe Bryant, the high school wunderkind from Philadelphia, who similarly made the jump from his Lower Merion high school to the NBA's Los Angeles Lakers, which drafted him with their thirteenth overall pick in the 1996 NBA Draft. As the son of former NBA player Joe Bryant, he was obviously built for that pro life, but he was so young when he was drafted that his parents had to legally co-sign his first NBA contract because he was only seventeen years old.

LeBron James, the NBA's all-time leading scorer, who a growing chorus of fans and pundits think is the greatest player of all time, didn't play a single game of college basketball and was drafted straight out of St. Vincent-St. Mary high school by his hometown NBA team, the Cleveland Cavaliers. In fact, if you were to put together an all-time starting lineup of players that were drafted directly out of high school (Kevin Garnett, Tracy McGrady, LeBron James, Kobe Bryant, Dwight Howard) and have them compete against a starting team who played NCAA college basketball, one could argue that the squad coming out of the high school pipeline might be victorious.

30

SNEAKERS OR A BURGER AND FRIES?

Today's basketball sneakers are very costly for your average person. Whether you are ready and eager to purchase staple performance basketball shoes from any of the classic top-selling brands like Nike, Adidas, Puma, the less visible classic New Balance or Converse brands, or the newer emerging brands like Under Armour and Li Ning, it can easily set you back a few hundred dollars. In fact, the average MSRP price of a basketball shoe is just over US$133.50, with high-tops typically costing in the high one hundreds, more than mid-tops and low-tops. And we're not even talking about the online sneaker resale market, where it's no secret that you might have to sell your primary residence and/or a few kidneys to be able to afford something like the "Dynasty Collection," which consists of six pairs of Michael Jordan's game-worn championship game–clinching sneakers and sold for $8 million at Sotheby's in 2024. We're just talking about buying your average everyday pair of basketball shoes to play in.

Enter legendary ex-NBA point guard and two-time NBA All-Star Stephon Marbury. Marbury's exploits on the court, from his high school and college days straight through to the end of his pro career, were epic. He went from being New York State's "Mr. Basketball" and a McDonald's All-American in high school to playing only one season of college ball at Georgia Tech, scoring nearly nineteen points per game, then was drafted fourth overall by the Minnesota Timberwolves in the 1996 NBA Draft. Marbury enjoyed a very productive thirteen-year career that saw him play for five different teams and earn over $100 million in salary before heading off to China in 2010 to continue his career there for another nine years. There, he enjoys demigod status. Not only did he win three Chinese Basketball Association championships with his club team, the Beijing Ducks, in 2012, 2014, and 2015, but his influence in China also earned him citizenship, and there's a permanent statue of him in Beijing.

But it's his off-the-court exploits and entry into the sneaker game that might arguably be his most memorable contribution to the game of basketball. In a nutshell, Marbury always privately wondered why basketball shoe prices were so high and how that might impact low-income racialized kids like himself who grew up poor in Brooklyn. Marbury always felt that high basketball sneaker price points made the game feel inaccessible, and he recalled his mother Mabel struggling to justify paying $65 for what were considered pricey Air Jordans back in 1985 (adjusted for inflation, using the consumer price index, $65 in 1985 amounts to $190.26 in 2024).

Fast forward twenty-one years, and Marbury made it part of his life's mission to ensure that all basketball players, regardless of class positioning, could access cheaper shoes to play in, so he partnered up with the owners of Steve & Barry's University Sportswear to manufacture a sneaker called the "Starbury" that retailed for only $14.98. In September 2006, they launched their first basketball shoe, "the Starbury One," and followed that with other basketball shoes in the line: the Air Force One–styled "Starbury Crossovers," "Starbury SXM," and the "Starbury Cyclones." The basketball sneaker line was manufactured in China, and if you look closely at Marbury's head, you'll see the Starbury logo tattooed there. Marbury wore these Chinese-manufactured shoes in his New York Knick games, and other players like NBA legend Steve Francis wore them too.

To this day, there's no exact publicly available forensic audit on the profit margins of the Starbury basketball shoes that were obviously super cheap to produce, but the company reportedly made millions of dollars, and those who wore the shoe say that it was a surprisingly good product to play in, especially given the price point. However, by 2008, Steve & Barry's filed for bankruptcy, and the shoes were no longer commercially available at retail stores by 2009. But these shoes and the hype surrounding them weren't gone for good, since six years later, in 2015, Marbury rebooted the company, and in 2016 the Starburys reentered the sneaker marketplace, this time with far less fanfare. You can still find Starburys on the vintage resale market and on popular e-tailers like Ebay, and they are all mostly still quite cheap.

31 HOOP MOM

With the rise in growth and popularity of women's basketball globally, with WNBA TV ratings going up six-fold from 2022 to 2024, the role of the basketball mom has taken some interesting turns too.

What isn't talked about enough is the journey undertaken by those women who choose to have children when their playing days are over, especially when those children want to follow in the footsteps of their mother and play basketball. The juggling act of helping to run a stable household off the court while managing a basketball playing kid's gruelling school and Amateur Athletic Union schedule in the classroom and on the court is a whole other ball of wax.

And then there's Pam McGee. She's an iconoclast and a permanent fixture in the basketball annals due to her success in the NCAA, WNBA, and playing for her country (the U.S.). In college, she won back-to-back championships at the University of Southern California in 1983 and 1984, and then won a gold medal at the 1984 Los Angeles Summer Olympics for the U.S. In the WNBA, she played during the late 1990s for the Los Angeles Sparks and Sacramento Monarchs. McGee also just happens to be the first WNBA player and mother to have kids play in the NBA and WNBA, and she makes up one half of the first mother-son duo to win Olympic gold medals. McGee's son, JaVale, won a gold medal at the 2020 Summer Olympics playing for the U.S., and he also won three NBA championships, two as a member of the Golden State Warriors (2017, 2018) and one with the Los Angeles Lakers (2020).

McGee's daughter, Imani McGee-Stafford, was a first-round draft pick by the Chicago Sky in the 2016 WNBA draft and made the WNBA All-Rookie team. She's also had stints with the Atlanta Dream and the Dallas Wings and has played overseas in Israel, China, Turkey, and Australia.

32
SHORT PEOPLE GOT MO' REASON TO LIVE

When basketball enthusiasts and pundits think of high-flying dunkers that have rattled rims and stolen fans' hearts since the NBA's inception, their knee-jerk response is almost always to reference some of the more obvious phenoms with good height who demonstrate a dazzling and wide array of dunks. Despite standing at a mere 5'6", Spud Webb, one of the shortest players in NBA history, is also the shortest NBA player to ever win the NBA Slam Dunk Contest in 1986.

When we think of NBA Slam Dunk Contest winners, we think of NBA Hall of Famers Vince Carter and Dominique Wilkins, silky-smooth shooting guard Zach LaVine, or Hall of Famer and Philadelphia 76ers great Julius "Dr. J" Erving. All of these players' heights fall in that 6'6"–6'9" sweet spot that many critics argue is the perfect height to take flight and create some magic in the air while pulling off a great dunk. The "white men can't jump" mantra has been challenged a few times with two smallish white guards, the 6'7" Brent Barry and 6'2" Mac McClung, both winning the NBA Slam Dunk Contest, in 2004 and 2023 respectively. Likewise, the accompanying "short guys can't dunk" vibe that has permeated a sport like basketball that rewards height through and through has also been challenged on numerous occasions.

By today's standards, the dunks Spud Webb executed against his teammate and NBA Slam Dunk Contest finalist Dominique Wilkins are pedestrian: an off-the-backboard one-handed jam, a 360-degree one-handed dunk, a reverse double-pump slam. But that's not the point. The point here is that it is a lot more challenging for a player who measures a few inches over five feet to pull off enough dazzling dunks to win a high-profile dunk competition. Twenty years later, 5'9" point guard Nate Robinson won his first of three NBA Slam Dunk Contests. Now, did a few of his dunk competition wins feel more like a sideshow or spectacle where high marks were given by the judges not so much for the degree of difficulty of the dunks but for the mere fact that a shorter player was pulling off some pretty amazing dunks? Absolutely.

33

LET'S GET PHYSICAL

Basketball is not considered a full-contact sport, but things can get downright physical when players are "boxing out" their opponents to grab a rebound, taking charges to draw offensive fouls, going up for dunks over their opponent, or when the offensive player drives to the hoop and gets fouled aggressively to prevent the opportunity for a three-point play or an "and-one" (where a player scores a basket, gets fouled, and then hits the free throw to total three points).

With elbows and arms flailing around throughout the course of an entire game, it's generally not in the best interest of players with poor eyesight to wear glasses unless absolutely necessary because they might get knocked off their face. Wearing contact lenses is a good and less hazardous option.

While a player might occasionally wear protective goggles after suffering an eye injury or for vision correction, with modern advances in eye care few players of today will wear goggles like NBA Hall of Famer Kareem Abdul-Jabbar or four-time NBA champ Horace Grant did throughout their careers and will opt for disposable contact lenses.

And then you have the curious case of four-time NBA champion and league executive Kurt Rambis, who enjoyed a fourteen-year career mainly in the 1980s wearing thick black horn-rimmed glasses reminiscent of Clark Kent — which was his nickname. No NBA player since the Greek-American Rambis retired in 1995 has played full seasons wearing glasses for vision correction like he did. He was near-sighted. However, a number of players have worn protective goggles (Jalen Smith, James Worthy, Horace Grant), mostly because it's awkward to play in glasses at that level, and it looks aesthetically out of place. Rambis's eyewear had a piece of rubber in the middle that looked like some geeked-out adhesive tape used to keep the glasses intact, and the glasses had to meet strict safety standards to ensure they didn't pose a risk to the other players on the court or the player wearing them. Rambis's rugged style of play, which included crashing the boards, committing hard fouls, and diving for loose balls with glasses on and fully intact, further cemented his cult status in NBA and Lakers history.

34 NBA, CIA

America almost always expects to win gold medals in basketball at the Olympic games, given the country's sheer dominance of the sport, the elite-level domestic Amateur Athletic Union circuits it houses, and that it's home to the most competitive league in the world.

When the Americans lost for the first time ever at the 1972 Olympics in Munich to Russia in the gold medal game by a score of 51–50, it sent shockwaves throughout the world, so much so that even the CIA looked into the game's controversial ending and result. The defeat came on the heels of the Munich Massacre, in which Palestinian terrorists killed eleven Israeli athletes just five days before the game, and there was all kinds of bumbling by the referees as they lost track of time outs. The teams had to replay the final three seconds of the game a few times over. A declassified investigative CIA memo later revealed that there was bias in the Fédération Internationale de Basketball jury's decision after the U.S. protested and appealed the game's result and even suggested there was foul play amongst the referees, who allegedly turned a blind eye to foul calls when they were supposed to go against the Russians. "Belov was guilty of fouling two Americans on his drive for the [winning] basket," read the report.

35 THE TWO WORLDS OF BASKETBALL

Many basketball players speak of the feeling of peace when they get out on the court to play in between the lines of the ninety-four-foot court. In the history of the NBA, a few players have made bold adjustments to their names, perhaps to reflect this sentiment.

Despite the big business behind the sport, basketball is still very much a game, and it can provide a temporary escape from the worldly ills that plague humanity.

From the mid-1970s into the 1980s, NBA legend Lloyd Bernard Free lit up opponents with his dazzling footwork, pinpoint jump shots, and high vertical jump, which allowed him to pull off 360-degree dunks despite being only 6'3". To reflect his free-thinking ways and playing style, in 1981 he legally changed his given name to World and became known as World B. Free, a name that said something without saying much.

Likewise, Ron Artest, one of the toughest, most hard-nosed defensive players of his era and an avowed free thinker who won a 2010 championship with the Kobe Bryant–led Los Angeles Lakers, changed his name to Metta World Peace in 2011. Despite his quirky and mildly eccentric ways, his name change was ultimately meant to drive home a salient point to humanity. He explained, "Metta is going to be the first name, and it means like friendship, love, and kindness" in Buddhism. "World Peace is going to be the last name, so everybody can get ready to buy their World Peace jerseys."

36
WHITE PRIVILEGE

When famed NBA champion point guard Kyrie Irving debuted his Anta Kai 1 "Chief Hélà" sneakers, his signature basketball shoe with Chinese athletic brand Anta Sports, during the 2024 NBA playoffs, many basketball players and sneaker enthusiasts high-fived one another. Essentially, in one fell on-court swoop, he was able to pay homage to his Native American heritage on his mother's side and do so in the most fashion-forward way imaginable.

NBA onlookers and cultural activists noted the shoes' distinct tassels, a feature that mimicked the moccasins worn by some Native Americans, and the slick brown suede. Modern basketball players have become fashion paragons, with some feeling like they are equally as attuned to their stat sheet numbers as they are to their style ratings. Certainly, sporting unique, exclusive, and colourful footwear is a strong part of that. This time around, Kyrie's on-court sneaker performance was intended to match the intensity of his cultural roots and attachments and his Dallas Mavericks team play as they made a deep run in the 2024–25 playoffs, eventually losing in the finals to the Boston Celtics.

This bedazzling display of fashion-meets-basketball-culture on the feet of NBA players would not have been possible just six years before. It was only in 2018 that the NBA allowed its players to be more fashion-conscious and expressive on the court and to wear multicoloured shoes. From the NBA's inception in 1949 straight through to 2018, you would have noticed that players routinely performed in majority white sneakers. The league's rules on sneaker decorum stated that the shoes had to be 51 percent white (dubbed the "51 Percent Rule"), and the only colour allowance was that players could wear shoes sporting the team's colour, tied to home and away games.

And then came Michael Jeffrey Jordan. Arguably the greatest player of all time, Jordan had something to do with chipping away at this rule, since during the 1984–85 season his Royal Airness was playing in his own signature Air Jordan red-and-black shoes. The NBA sent him a letter warning him going against this colour code and banning his Air Jordans that carried no traces of white. Jordan's signature debut red-and-black Air Jordans ended up selling into the multi-millions for Nike, which naturally lapped up and took full advantage of all of this attention.

By 2012, the NBA's theme nights allowed for more colourful collaborations across sneaker brands to commemorate important days and events like Black History Month, during which sporting white-leaning sneakers just wouldn't cut it. Shoes that appeared in team colours were allowed by the late 2000s, so, for example, Los Angeles Lakers players could wear all yellow or purple shoes with no pushback from the league. Then, by 2018, the NBA got rid of the colour restrictions and opened up the floodgates to mix and match colours to suit players' own fancy, within reason. In the end, white sneaker supremacy died a slow, painful death after Jordan left his stamp on the league, and if we're to be completely honest, it's not exactly a rule that could survive today's social media–fuelled, multihued sneaker culture output that has become so prevalent in the game.

37
DRAFT HER, IT, AND THAT?

In 1977, 6'3" centre and Delta State University women's basketball phenom Lusia Harris was drafted by the New Orleans Jazz of the NBA in the seventh round with the 137th overall pick.

The only issue here is that the NBA is a men's league. So how did Harris become the first and only woman officially drafted by a male NBA team? Well, the pick had something to do with the older NBA Draft structure, which at that time featured eight full rounds of draft picks. There was even a time when the NBA Draft went a full twenty-one rounds, in 1960 and 1968! Today, the NBA Draft only carries two rounds, with sixty draft picks in total, and for good reason.

The 1977 NBA Draft will go down in history as the most bizarre because the owners were no longer interested in participating in any more marathon eight-round drafts and concocted a scheme to expose the absurdity of it all. They did this in the later rounds, drafting all kinds of people, things, and objects that had nothing to do with men's basketball. Cartoon character Scooby-Doo was drafted, as was decathlete Bruce Jenner. A wooden chair owned by Jerry West's mother was drafted by the Lakers, and the Boston Celtics drafted their waterboy. And the Jazz drafting Harris, who was pregnant at the time, with the 137th pick, was what kick-started this silent protest. Despite the sheer ridiculousness of the 1977 NBA Draft process, amazingly, the league didn't reduce the draft to two rounds until twelve years later in 1989. In the end, Harris declined the opportunity to test her mettle in the NBA. NBA Draft oddities notwithstanding, Harris enjoyed a solid career in the women's game, mostly at the amateur sports level, including playing on the 1976 USA women's basketball team that took home the silver medal at the Olympics.

38

BALLING ABILITIES

NBA shooting guard Gerald Green had a long and productive fifteen-year career, highlighted by winning the 2007 NBA All-Star Game's slam dunk competition while averaging a respectable 9.7 points per game in his career. What few knew is that while Green was delivering tantalizing highlight reel dunks and knocking down jump shots during NBA regular season and playoff games, he was only playing with nine fingers.

As an eleven-year-old, Green joined his brother in a jumping competition, and he just happened to be wearing a ring on his right-hand finger. When he jumped up, the ring caught a nail, and his full finger was almost torn off. When he went to the doctor, they were not able to save the full finger, so they partially amputated his right ring finger. Green had to quickly learn to adjust his shooting form using his index finger, middle finger, and thumb to get the ball off in the same way. And it clearly worked, since his career free throw percentage and three-point field goal percentage were 80.1 and 36.1 respectively.

Some notable WNBA superstars like former Indiana Fever small forward Tamika Catchings have also had to overcome physical disabilities or impairments to compete and thrive at the highest level. Catchings was born with severe hearing loss in both ears, wore hearing aids, and relied on lip reading while on her way to becoming one of the greatest and most decorated players in women's basketball herstory, including winning an NCAA championship with the Tennessee Lady Volunteers and a WNBA championship with the Fever, where she was a ten-time all-star.

39 ROOFTOP, BLACKTOP

In North America, basketball courts are widely accessible and can mostly be found in public parks, on school and college facilities, in recreation centres, residential areas, or private gyms and clubs. Finding open space with a hoop to play this beautiful game is never an issue.

As a result, playing basketball on rooftops is just never presented as an option. In China, on the other hand, due to population density challenges in urban areas, rooftop basketball courts are quite popular, especially in cities like Beijing and Shanghai where open space is very limited. These rooftop courts are often used for recreational basketball games and they provide a unique and scenic location for playing sports, offering unique views of the city skyline. Choi Hung Estate Rooftop Basketball Court is one of Hong

Kong's most iconic urban photography spots, and rooftop courts have become a symbol of urban leisure, coupled with progressive urban planning and a creative use of space in densely populated Chinese cities.

40

AND1 × THE GREATEST DUNKER ALIVE

When people think of AND1, they almost singularly recall streetball and mixtape culture and hark back to the 1980s and 1990s, when street basketball players like Rafer "Skip to My Lou" Alston, Grayson "the Professor" Boucher, or Larry "Bone Collector" Williams pulled off rare circus-like basketball tricks on the court and basketball's pure entertainment value hit one of its peaks.

Likewise, when people think of the limited edition AND1 Tai Chi shoes, they are not mentioning those shoes in the same sentence as arguably the greatest dunker of all-time, Vince Carter, a first-ballot NBA Hall of Famer. In the realm of high-performance basketball sneakers, it's more like Tai Who? As strange as it sounds, Carter, the world's greatest dunk maestro, won the only NBA dunk competition he ever entered in 2000 wearing obscure, kitschy AND1 brand shoes. And the backstory behind how he ended up wearing AND1s is even weirder, since this was a time before there was such a thing as Instagram and TikTok virality, and his rarefied air-defying elbow-locked-in-rim dunks still went analogue viral.

In the history of basketball shoes, AND1 carries this highly unicorn outlier history, since it was a company started by Seth Berger, Tom Austin, and Jay Coen Gilbert, Wharton School (University of Pennsylvania) business grads. And the company first gained its reputation in 1993 not through sneakers but through selling their comedic slogan-driven trash talk T-shirt lines ("Pass. Save yourself the embarrassment," "Go to church. Pray you don't guard me"). When they entered the shoe game, their sneakers were clunky, unattractive, and cheaper ($75) than the more popular Nike, Adidas, and Reebok brands.

When Vince Carter was drafted by the Toronto Raptors in 1998, he signed a deal with Puma because they offered him a lucrative ten-year, fifty-million-dollar contract and also offered him a signature shoe. When word spread that outside of the fiscal benefits, Carter was not thrilled with Puma, he now had to get out of the contract. What that also meant was that if he were to entertain offers from Nike, Adidas, or Reebok, they would be on the hook to buy out the rest of his contract from Puma. So, while Carter continued on this sneaker purgatory journey, with his next shoe deal up in the air in his camp, he started to transform the league with his human-highlight-reel in-game dunks.

In 2000, the NBA got set to stage its glitzy NBA All-Star Slam Dunk Contest dunk-off, one of the highlights of the annual NBA All-Star weekend. It was also during that year that AND1 launched their Tai Chi line. Carter was the leading vote getter for the 2000 game, racking up 1,911,973 votes from fans, and given his public exit strategy with Puma, he was allowed to wear any sneaker brand he wanted to in the dunk competition because he didn't currently have a deal. AND1 was always super-savvy when it came to seeding out new shoes and apparel products to potential clients, and they had always been shipping new AND1 shoes and products to Carter. Given that Carter didn't have a shoe deal, he ended up wearing AND1s to play in both the NBA All-Star Game and in the dunk competition.

During the high-visibility dunk competition, Carter sported his cushy new size 16 AND1 Tai Chis with the number 15 on the back of his sneaker. And the rest, as they say, is history. In one of the most electrifying dunk contests in the history of the game, Carter carried out a series of iconic in-competition dunks: a reverse 360-degree windmill, a between-the-legs, two-handed reverse windmill, and an elbow-hang "honey dip" dunk that future generations of dunkers have been mimicking ever since.

After pulling off that never-before-seen dunk, he gestured to the assembled audience and TV crew and declared, "It's over," since he knew that his competitors, Houston Rockets point guard Steve Francis and his Toronto Raptors teammate and first cousin Tracy McGrady, could not match his dunk repertoire. That same summer, Carter, now signed with sneaker powerhouse Nike, continued his gravity-defying ways at the 2000 Sydney Olympics by jumping over the head of 7'2" French centre Frédéric Weis.

41

UNDER ARMOUR, OVER ACHIEVER

The American sporting apparel brand Under Armour has become synonymous with Golden State Warriors shooting guard Steph Curry, the greatest three-point shooter in the history of basketball.

Before Curry signed with Under Armour in 2013, the brand was languishing in relative obscurity when it came to appealing to basketball players and youth culture types. When Curry came on board, his signature shoe line and apparel captured the imagination of players from across the skill and global spectrum who all wanted to be like Steph, given his four NBA championships, record-breaking three-point shooting prowess, and two-time NBA Three-Point Contest wins. In 2020, Curry signed a new long-term contract with Under Armour, which included an equity stake in the company and the establishment of the Curry Brand, which focuses on basketball performance and initiatives to support underserved communities. The more curious and ironic side to this fantastic corporate connection is that it wasn't even supposed to happen.

In 2009, Curry had originally signed with Nike after being drafted seventh overall in the NBA Draft Lottery, coming out of Davidson University. His first sneaker deal with Nike was a no-brainer given their track record of marketing, branding, and positioning their A-list athletes for the success that comes with representing the swoosh. Fast forward to 2013, and the ball was in Nike's court to re-sign Curry to a lucrative deal, given that he'd led the Warriors to the Western Conference semifinals that year, he'd worn Nike throughout his college years at Davidson and his four years in the league, and his godfather worked for Nike. Light work for Nike, right?

Well, not exactly. Reportedly, the relationship between Curry and Nike soured during a pitch meeting in 2013, when, according to Steph's father, NBA veteran Dell Curry, various missteps took place, including beginning the meeting by mispronouncing Curry's given name. Then, later on in the meeting, the Nike official showed a PowerPoint presentation slide with the wrong athlete's name (Kevin Durant) on it, another sloppy administrative error.

Curry reportedly just didn't feel valued enough or that he would have received a signature shoe deal like Nike's other A-listers, LeBron James, Kevin Durant, or Anthony Davis. These incidents played a significant role in Curry's decision to leave Nike and sign with Under Armour later that year. The sales of Curry Brand shoes increased Under Armour's profits twenty-fold since his signing — which is exactly what happens when you do business with the guy who revolutionized the sport of basketball with his otherworldly three-point shooting prowess.

42
AMAZONIAN

Only one female seven-footer has played in the WNBA. The late Polish centre Margo Dydek, who stood 7'2", played for the Utah Starzz/San Antonio Silver Stars, the Connecticut Sun, and the Los Angeles Sparks, where she was a two-time WNBA league All-Star and became the WNBA's all time block leader at 877, a record that still stands. Dydek died tragically while pregnant with her third child, experiencing cardiac arrest, going into a coma, and never regaining consciousness. She was remembered as a giant ambassador of the game, both on and off the court during her post-playing days as a coach.

The vast majority of the other giants in women's basketball, most of whom ended up hooping in the WNBA, come from countries outside of the West, with few exceptions. Chinese player Han Xu and Hungarian pro player Bernadett Határ were both listed at 7'0" but were actually 6'10" when measured, which mirrors the height-boosting ritual that happens in the men's game. Other international players, like 6'9" three-time Olympic medalist and Russian star Maria Stepanova or 6'8" Australian baller Liz Cambage, who once scored fifty-three points in a WNBA game, a league single-game scoring record, were nearly unstoppable when it came to their low-post game, rebounding, and blocking shots due to their significant height advantage; the average height of a WNBA player is six feet.

Certainly one the most recognizable and decorated female basketball bigs of all time is 6'9" centre Brittney Griner, due to a confluence of factors, beginning with her on-court accolades (2012 NCAA Champion and two-time player of the year with Baylor University, 2014 WNBA champion with the Phoenix Mercury, three-time Olympic gold medalist), advocacy for LGBTQIA+ rights (she came out in 2013 and wrote a compelling memoir, *In My Skin*, which details that process), and off-court issues (in 2022 she was charged with drug possession in Russia in a case that ultimately led to her release in a high-profile prisoner exchange).

43

THAT BLOODY MASCOT

The NBA's Denver Nuggets' mascot, Rocky the mountain lion, is one of the most entertaining professional mascots in the NBA and across all team sports. He is wildly entertaining and gets paid big bucks, raking in a $625,000 a year salary for his efforts. Rocky (actor/performer Kenn Solomon) has played Rocky for thirty-plus years and has consistently raised the bar when it comes to his on-court acrobatics and antics — almost to the point of dying. In 2013, the Nuggets decided to have Rocky enter the Pepsi Center Court arena by air dropping him onto the court with a harness for the home opener against the Portland Trail Blazers. During the entire drop from high up in the rafters, all the way down to the floor of the court, Rocky's body looked limp and lifeless, and he collapsed on the floor. Apparently, the harness had cut off his circulation during the drop, and the question, which still gets asked to this day when we watch our favourite lovable, huggable mascots pulling off death-defying stunts to keep us basketball fans entertained, is "how much is too much?"

That was not Rocky's first brush with serious injury, since he once also parachuted into the Nuggets arena, got stuck in the sky-high ceiling, and was left there dangling until arena staff were able to rescue him from any real-life danger.

44

BLACK FIVES

Black men have dominated the mainstream sport of basketball since it was officially integrated in 1950. By the late 1950s and early 1960s, as the game became more fully integrated, Black players began filling up many of the roster spots in the NBA, and none of this would have been possible without the early innovations and inventions of the Black Fives. The Black Fives era refers to the period in basketball history before the racial integration of professional leagues, spanning roughly the early 1900s to the late 1940s. During that time, African American players played in segregated leagues, and their basketball teams, known as "Black Fives" (the fives referenced the five starting players on each team) journeyed throughout the U.S. Some of the more notable teams included the New

York Renaissance (Rens), established in 1923, one of the most successful and well-known Black Fives teams. They won numerous championships and defeated many of the top white teams of their time.

The Harlem Globetrotters, founded in 1926, actually started out as a competitive team but then became famous for their entertaining style of play, combining athleticism and humour. The Black Fives era was significant in promoting basketball within African American communities and providing opportunities for Black athletes to showcase their talents. These teams laid down the foundation for the integration of pro basketball leagues. The integration of professional basketball began with the signing of African American players by the National Basketball League in the late 1940s. It later merged with the all-white Basketball Association of America to form the NBA.

Claude Johnson, founder of the Black Fives Foundation, which works to preserve and promote the history of this era through research, exhibitions, and educational programs, says that the history and legacy of the Black Fives is something that all basketball enthusiasts should read more about to gain a better understanding of American history and Black people's position within it.

"So why not know the history? Not just play and watch the game, but know the history. LeBron is King James, but Will Anthony Madden was the king of Black basketball in the 1910s and is buried in an unmarked grave. So, what does that say?"

45

NO DUNKING, PLEASE

The term "slam dunk" was coined by Lakers broadcaster Chick Hearn to describe the action of a basketball player slamming the ball down into the rim for two points. It's the highest-percentage shot in basketball and arguably the shot that generates the most excitement at games due to the athleticism and ferocity needed to execute it. So, it's hard to believe that dunking was banned in the NCAA and in high school sports from 1967 to 1976.

The ban was largely attributed to the dominance of UCLA centre and phenomenon Lew Alcindor (who changed his name to Kareem Abdul-Jabbar on January 1, 1971, after his conversion to Islam), who was so dominant and skilled at 7'2" that the league had to drum up a rule to slow him down and prevent the future dominance of any more supremely tall, lanky, and skilled Alcindoresque players. In fact, the no-dunking rule was sometimes referred to as the "Lew Alcindor rule."

Others attributed the dunking ban to racism, since at the time most of the prominent dunkers in college basketball were Black, and the ban took place less than a year after the 1966 NCAA University Division basketball championship game in which the Texas Western College team (now called the University of Texas at El Paso) with an all-Black starting lineup beat the all-white University of Kentucky team led by coach Adolph Rupp, who was reluctant to recruit Black players, to win the national championship. That was the first time an all-Black team won the NCAA championship before the game began to become more integrated in the late 1960s.

46 MARCH MADNESS

When the final sixty-four teams are picked to play in the annual NCAA men's tournament, dubbed March Madness, partly due to its flurry of high-intensity elimination games played in March, pitting obscure teams from small conferences against top-ranked blue-blood Power 5 conference teams, major upsets have become the norm.

And it's mostly in the first round of the NCAA Tournament that these David versus Goliath matchups between the top teams — ranked from one to sixteen — across four different brackets really comes to life. Since the NCAA tournament expanded to sixty-four teams in 1985, only two sixteen-seed teams have ever pulled off a huge upset of a one seed. In 2018, during the opening round of the south region game, the sixteenth-seeded UMBC (University of Maryland, Baltimore County) Retrievers upset the highly favoured University of Virginia Cavaliers, winning by twenty points, 74–54. Prior to 2018, no sixteen-seed had ever beaten a number one seed in 135 tries. What made this upset so jarring was that UMBC was a 20.5-point underdog yet ended up winning by that much.

Five years later, in 2023, only the second recorded sixteen-seed upset of a number one seed happened when Fairleigh Dickinson upset the number-one-ranked Purdue Boilermakers, led by 2023 NCAA player of the year and now NBA centre, 7'4" Zach Edey, despite going into the game as 23.5-point underdogs.

47

FOULING OUT, NAH

In basketball, players receiving touch and reach-in fouls, getting technical fouls for cursing out a referee, or dishing out intentional fouls to prevent their opponents from scoring easy baskets like a layup or dunk is as old as the pyramids.

Committing a shooting foul is never good, because once the foul is committed, the player who got fouled in the act of shooting gets to shoot free throws. Fouling shooters who are taking a three-point shot attempt is the absolute worst defensive act one can commit because it means the player who got fouled gets to shoot three free throws. That's potentially giving away three easy points to the opponent.

Wilt Chamberlain, one of the greatest NBA players of all time, never fouled out of a single NBA game in his entire career (a player fouls out after committing six personal fouls). This all seems impossible considering he was physically imposing at 7'1" and 270 pounds. His whole method was to punish players on the boards, glass, and in the paint, on both sides of the floor, whether it be backing opposing players down in the post for low-post moves and dunks or blocking and swatting away any attempts by the offensive player to score. That typically draws many fouls. And it's not like he had a short career, either, unlike most players (the average NBA career lasts 4.5 years, though for first-round draft picks like Chamberlain, careers typically average between eight to ten years). Chamberlain actually played a full fourteen years in the NBA, and over twelve hundred games, which means plenty of time to foul out of games!

Given that basketball is as physical a sport as any, how was it possible for Chamberlain to limit his fouls like that? It's largely because he had a very rare combination of speed, athleticism, size, and strength, coupled with a high basketball IQ and a calculated approach to playing defence. At his size, he was able to clear out so much space on the court that he could rebound and defend opponents with ease without fouling. Also, utilizing his high basketball IQ often meant that his detailed footwork allowed him to navigate and manoeuvre his body around opponents while still playing very strict defence.

Chamberlain's long arms and reach also allowed him to block shots at a far enough distance from his opponents to limit contact, and his in-game discipline and poise meant that he knew he would be hurting his team quite badly if he fouled out.

48

SHOOT. SCORE (A LOT). REPEAT.

Today's professional basketball games are notorious for racking up sky-high point totals. The NBA now enjoys the claim of being the highest-scoring league in all of professional sports, with games averaging over 114 points per game by 2024. But this wasn't always the case. In fact, the lowest-scoring NBA game in history occurred in 1950 when the Fort Wayne Pistons defeated the Minneapolis Lakers with a final score of 19–18. In today's NBA, those scoring totals would be surpassed within the first five minutes of most games. The low-scoring games of yesteryear can be largely attributed to the fact that there was no three-point line, since that shot was only implemented in 1979–80 and was heavily influenced by the popular competing American Basketball Association; it had involved three-point shooting, which was a success both with the players and the fans. Also, the implementation of the twenty-four-second shot clock at the start of the 1954–55 season meant that players could not waste time running out the clock, holding up the game, and risk turning the ball over to the opposing team if they did not get a shot up in time.

When you watch black-and-white footage of most NBA games before 1954, the pace is often slow and plodding, and with good reason; there was no shot clock in place to force the issue of scoring! In the lowest-scoring game in NBA history, the Pistons intentionally dribbled around the court for minutes on end, with no intention to shoot much, taking full advantage of the fact that there was no shot clock. This strategy was mostly to nullify the scoring exploits of opposing centre George Mikan of the Los Angeles Lakers, a dominant offensive force. And it was also this particular game that got officials thinking about the possibility of adding a shot clock to the league's rule repertoire.

Fast-forward to the NBA's modern era, and not only is there now arguably too much of a focus on scoring and less attention paid to defence, but you would have to go way back to the 2012–13 season to find the last time NBA games averaged less than a hundred points per game. You can call it the Splash Brothers effect, since it was during the 2012–13 season that the greatest three-point shooter of all time, Golden State Warriors guard Steph Curry, alongside his backcourt teammate, shooting guard Klay Thompson, hit the ground running as the best pure three-point shooting duo of all time.

Also during that season, Curry eclipsed Hall of Famer Ray Allen's record of 269 three-pointers in a regular season by three (272). NBA scoring averages enjoyed a sustained increase when this Curry-esque formula of teams shooting a few dozen threes a game started, and it led to the Golden State Warriors' hot streak of three NBA championships in four years, beginning in the 2014–15 season by utilizing this high-powered offensive scoring formula.

49

720 DEGREES OF FUN

In basketball, when a player throws down a dunk of any stripe — one-handed, two-handed, reverse, windmill, East Bay — one could argue that it is by far the easiest and splashiest way to score two points, as compared with hitting a layup or a midrange jump shot.

Long before social media existed, the quickest way to get an off-court viral moment was to throw down a fancy dunk that carried a high degree of difficulty. It's what earned players props and respect from their teammates, and especially fans, whose cheers grew exponentially louder when a high-flying dunk was executed. Within the range and wide spectrum of dunks, executing a 360-degree dunk was long considered to be the one with the highest measure of difficulty, a step up from slightly less difficult dunks like a windmill.

The 360-degree dunks were also rewarded during NBA All-Star game dunk competitions, often earning competitors perfect fifties. Skywalking North Carolina State guard David Thompson threw down the first 360-degree dunk in a game, in 1974, helping to make it a staple of TV highlight reels and in dunk contests during the golden era of the 1980s and 1990s. Hall of Famers Vince Carter and Kobe Bryant upped the ante in the late 1990s, with Carter in particular throwing down flurries of 360-degree dunks in games, radically shifting the view on how dunks can or should be executed. In particular, in the 2000 NBA Slam Dunk Contest, Carter threw down a 360-degree windmill that is still talked about to this day.

Just as all sports records are meant to be broken, so too were extreme A-list dunk repertoires. Fast-forward to 2006, when prolific streetballer Taurian Fontenette, known by his street alias, "the Air Up There," due to his otherworldly vertical jump and leaping ability, took flight in Houston, Texas, at an AND1 game and executed the first 720-degree dunk in a game. Fontenette was a former player in the AND1 Mixtape tour, and his execution of a 720-degree dunk, an incredibly rare and advanced move that involves completing two full rotations in the air before executing the dunk, carries a high degree of coordination, hang time, concentration, and athleticism. No one had ever seen that dunk accomplished at any level of competitive high school, college, or pro basketball.

After executing this jaw-dropping dunk, Fontenette became a bit of a cult figure, with all kinds of urban legends and folklore popping up about him executing that dunk a few more times, though there's no video evidence available anywhere. Once the North American media in particular got a hold of his dunking exploits, he did the major media circuit, including a spot on ESPN, and was even hired to pull off the dunk in a paid advertisement to promote a new DLP High Definition TV by Texas Instruments.

Many dunkers competing in dunk competitions have tried to mimic the dunk and failed, further cementing Fontenette as the certified dunk king of that rarefied air up there.

50
GIANTS OF AFRICA

In a sport that rewards height, it's been an open secret in modern day basketball from the high school and college level all the way to the NBA that Africa has become a fertile recruiting ground for scouts looking for "bigs" to play the centre position, which mostly means looking for players measuring at least seven feet.

Smart high school recruiters looking to get an insta-seven-footer have been scouring the continent since the 1980s, trying to luck out.

The South Sudanese are some of the tallest people in the world on average, particularly among the Nuer and Dinka tribes. It's also no surprise that a disproportionate number of sky-scraping seven-footers plying their trade in the most highly competitive basketball circuits in the world, including the NCAA and NBA, just happen to have African roots. The first continental African NBA player to play in the league was 6'11" centre Nigerian Hakeem Olajuwon, whose dominance at both the college (University of Houston) and pro levels (Houston Rockets), where he won championships, laid the groundwork for the influx of incredibly tall, skilled, and agile African basketball talents.

In more recent times, we're talking about everyone from Greek-Nigerian 2020 NBA champion Giannis Antetokounmpo and Cameroonian 2024 NBA MVP Joel Embiid all the way to half-Congolese 2023 NBA number one draft pick, 7'3" centre Victor Wembanyama, who most critics agree will eventually be one of the best basketball players the world has ever seen.

Given the globalization of the game, there is clearly something brewing on the African continent. Former Toronto Raptors president Masai Ujiri has slowly but surely become another giant of Africa — and it has nothing to do with his 6'4" height. As the first African-born general manager of a North American pro sports team, he stands out not only for leading the expansion Raptors to an NBA championship in 2019 but also for putting together a roster with three players (Serge Ibaka, OG Anunoby, and Pascal Siakam) who have African roots playing key roles.

The Nigerian-Kenyan Ujiri, who was born in the U.K., was a pro basketball player who plied his trade on the courts of Europe for six years before becoming the 2013 NBA Executive of the Year. He has quietly used his status to affect the development of the game in Africa and to trigger societal change off the court. And Ujiri is fervently hoping more players come out of Africa. Ujiri created his Giants of Africa foundation in 2003 to honour the work of his idol, the late freedom fighter Nelson Mandela. Its mission is to "use basketball as a means to educate and enrich the lives of African youth" and "to provide quality facilities, gear, and coaches with the goal of growing the game of basketball within Africa."

"We create awareness and support for underprivileged children and young adults through our camps, which place emphasis on hard work, accountability, honest living and positivity," says Ujiri. "We strive to create opportunity not only as a player, but in other related areas — urging African youth to Dream Big."

He is also director of the NBA's Basketball Without Borders Africa program, which promotes basketball throughout the continent, and has been one of the brains behind NBA Academy Africa, an elite basketball training centre in Senegal for the top male and female prospects from throughout Africa, the first of its kind on the continent. In November 2018, the NBA opened a new elite basketball training centre in Saly, Senegal, to serve as the primary training location for NBA Academy Africa prospects from across the continent.

51 VERTICALLY CHALLENGED

It's incredibly difficult to remain gainfully employed in pro basketball if you're listed under six feet. There are many reasons for favouring taller players; they enjoy a closer proximity to the standard ten-foot-tall basketball hoop and can score easy baskets, rebound missed shots, or block them. That being said, a small and mighty number of notable five-footers have made a mark on the NBA.

Basketball is a game based around height, for both genders. So while Muggsy Bogues gets all of the ink for playing in the NBA while standing at a mere 5'3", former Los Angeles Sparks, Indiana Fever, and Washington Mystics point guard Shannon Bobbitt, who stands at 5'2", one inch shorter than Bogues, is the shortest player in the history of the WNBA. And despite Bobbitt's relative obscurity in mainstream and malestream discussions about vertically challenged basketball pros, some parts of her career are just as, if not more storied than Bogues's. She won back-to-back (2006, 2007) NCAA college championships at the University of Tennessee before being drafted to the WNBA.

Despite 5'7" Spud Webb and 5'9" Nate Robinson winning the 1987 and 2004 NBA dunk competitions and 5'5" point guard Earl Boykins enjoying a solid thirteen-year career, the reality of the situation is that the vast majority of NBA players who stood under six feet tall have had very short careers. Why? It's because professional basketball players are among the tallest athletes in the world, with an average height of around 6'7". Most teams in the thirty-team league boast multiple players who measure in the 6'8"–7'-plus range. Basketball has never been a sport favourable to the vertically challenged, with few notable exceptions. No player under five feet has ever made the league, regardless of skill level. The closest would be Muggsy Bogues.

At five feet, three inches tall in shoes, Muggsy enjoyed a fourteen-year career (1987–2001) playing point guard for four different NBA franchises: Washington, Charlotte, Golden State, and Toronto, and recorded 146 career double-doubles. Muggsy just happened to run the point guard position for arguably one of the best high school basketball teams ever assembled, Dunbar High School, which featured a whole slew of future NBA players (Reggie Lewis, Reggie Williams, David Wingate). So one could say that he was prepared for the high-stakes, high-pressure professional basketball life since he was a youth.

Also, when it came to being tough and resilient, Muggsy was wired to overcome most obstacles put in front of him after having had to survive and witness violent incidents in his Baltimore neighbourhood while helping to support drug-addicted family members, so he was built tough. Consider this: Despite his stature, Bogues blocked thirty-nine shots throughout his career, including one on seven-foot centre Patrick Ewing.

52

VC, KENNY G

It may be next to impossible to believe that VC (Vince Carter), the greatest dunker of all time and an NBA Hall of Famer, could do anything but throw down nasty dunks that landed many of your poor basketball heroes on posters. But outside of the fifty-plus basketball scholarships Carter was offered out of high school as a basketball phenom named Florida's Mr. Basketball in 1995, he was also offered a music scholarship to attend Bethune-Cookman, a respected historically Black university in Daytona Beach, Florida.

Thankfully, he chose to pursue basketball at the University of North Carolina instead, where he became a consensus second-team NCAA All-American and led his team to back-to-back Final Four appearances.

Carter was a very good saxophonist throughout his school years and had been playing music since the sixth grade, inspired by his band director stepdad. Carter says, "Talk about the pressure of being good when your dad's the band director. I had to be in the first two or three chairs. Obviously, my goal was, if I'm going to do this, I'm going to be the best, so I was first or second chair always."

Carter also taught himself how to play the trombone and tuba. Had he accepted that music scholarship to Bethune-Cookman, who knows — we might have been talking about the next Charlie Parker. While Carter has been known to pick up the saxophone to play every so often, we're so glad he decided to stick to his "day job."

53

DUNKING DUNKETTE

The act of dunking a basketball is far less common in the women's game than it is in men's play. In fact, it's an absolute rarity. Former WNBA superstar Lisa Leslie is broadly known as the first woman to dunk in a professional basketball game, on July 30, 2002, during a WNBA game between the Los Angeles Sparks and the Miami Sol. Just slightly below major media sightlines, and eighteen years earlier, before TikTok, Instagram, and social media virality existed, Georgeann Wells pulled off this feat on December 21, 1984, while playing for West Virginia University in a game against the University of Charleston.

Standing at 6'7", Wells was a junior at the time, and her goal was to dunk in a game before she graduated. She and her coaches would work on dunks during practice, sometimes dunking up to twenty times to master her form. Despite no real precedent ever being set in the women's game to dunk the ball during a live action game, she just went for it and pulled off a one-handed dunk on a breakaway. Wells had hops!

54

LOWERED STANDARDS

While there isn't an official Women's Dunk Contest associated with major basketball leagues like the WNBA or NCAA, given that so few women in the history of the game have been able to dunk on the standardized ten-foot rims — only eight women have dunked in a WNBA game as of 2024 — there have been instances where the few women players who can dunk have entered male dunking competitions and won.

For example, at the prestigious 2004 McDonald's High School All-American Game, Candace Parker became the first woman to win the contest, though some critics considered her win to be a bit of a novelty given the lesser degree of difficulty of her dunks. "Her pedestrian dunks didn't advance equality or women's basketball," wrote

ESPN's contrarian Jason Whitlock. "Had a healthy boy completed the same dunks in an all-star dunk contest, he might've been booed off the court."

And still others, like NBA legend Shaquille O'Neal, are strong proponents of lowering the WNBA rims to allow for women to be able to dunk more easily and thus increase the excitement factor and interest in games. But the "lowering the rims for women" crowd has been scolded by women over the years for even daring to suggest such a thing. In 2018, former WNBA Players Association president Nneka Ogwumike shot down any notions about changing rim heights to appease women. "It's not logical to ask us to do that," she said. "We're constantly being compared to men. We have people excelling at a ten-foot rim. And now, you want us to lower the rim so we can continuously be compared, only to still be criticized. Because now you have someone like me who has done what she's done — now I have to relearn the game to appease people who don't want to watch it for what it is."

55

THE UN-GOAT (IN THREE-POINT SHOOTING)

Even GOATs have off nights. And nowhere was this more apparent than when Michael Jordan entered the NBA All-Star Game's three-point shooting contest in 1990. While Jordan was more celebrated and recognized for his midrange game, he entered the contest with the same daring bravado and panache that made him so dominant in other parts of the game when it came to scoring, despite the fact that his three-point shooting percentages in these early stages of his career were not good (in the first five seasons of his career his three-point percentage was under .300).

His Royal Airness put up a stinker in the 1990 NBA three-point contest, scoring the lowest number of points (five) ever since the contest's inception, a record that still stands to this day. Phoenix Suns shooting guard Devin

Booker has the highest NBA three-point contest total at thirty-seven, a feat he performed in 2021.

Naturally, Jordan didn't make it out of the first round of the competition, and he, along with the rest of the contestants, lost to the eventual winner, Jordan's Chicago Bulls teammate, shooting guard Craig Hodges.

56
GRANNY RULES

Interestingly, there has always been a tiny outlier nation of basketball players who prefer to shoot free throws using the "granny style" (underhand) technique, beginning with NBA legend Rick Barry.

Former NBA pro, NCAA champion at University of Nevada Las Vegas, and power forward Larry Johnson took on a "grandmama" character, where he dressed up like a grandmother, as part of a comedic Converse campaign in the 1990s to shill shoes. This superstar elderly female character portrayed by Johnson could dribble, rebound, and throw down dunks like there's no tomorrow. Based on the commercial series, no one knows if this fictional character could shoot free throws with pinpoint accuracy, but shooting free throws in today's modern era of basketball is pretty simple and straightforward. You stand at the line, hold the ball with your shooting hand above your shoulder, snap your wrist, and then heave the ball forward and up at the rim.

Despite the fact that 99.99 percent of basketball players shoot free throws using the overhead technique, Rick Barry insisted that his technique could help poor free throw shooters improve their accuracy. And as one of the greatest free throw shooters in the history of the game, with a near 90 percent accuracy rate over fourteen professional seasons, how could you argue with him?

"I really truly can't comprehend the aversion people have to trying something that could be very effective for them," he said.

Of the hundreds of thousands of basketball players to play the game at a high college or NBA level, apparently only former Houston Rockets centre Chinanu Onuaku and Barry's son Canyon received that memo and took it seriously; they both shot free throws underhanded in the NBA and college respectively, with Onuaku's shot experiencing a 13 percent improvement since using the technique over a short stint of six games in the NBA and Canyon shooting 80 percent over his four-year NCAA college career.

A few other players famously used the technique, such as Hall of Famer Wilt Chamberlain, who shot at an improved 61.3 percent in his dream 1961–62 season when he averaged 50.4 points per game and shot the highest free throw accuracy rate in his career. But he then abandoned the technique. Why? Because most men intimated that the granny style was for girls and women, given that women utilized the technique from the early 1900s to the late 1970s and early 1980s. Back then, women were perceived to have less arm strength than men, so this was the way to address that supposed shortcoming. And clearly that mythology has been debunked if not outright annihilated in recent times.

57

DRIBBLING FAUX PAS

We often marvel at the dribbling and ballhandling skills of players like Pistol Pete Maravich or Kyrie Irving, point guards who are able to dribble and manipulate the ball at lightning-quick speeds and with flair while creating space and navigating through and around defences.

Other point guards like Tim Hardaway and Allen Iverson are also celebrated for their ability to pull off rare and skilled crossover moves that often leave defenders lying in their wake. So, then, it's quite hard to imagine that basketball did not even involve dribbling in its infancy. Dribbling was not a part of the original thirteen rules of basketball invented by Dr. James Naismith, so in the earliest days of the game players would just pass the ball to one another to be caught, stand in place, and then repeat that action with their teammates. Or the player could bounce the ball one time before passing it.

Despite the invention of basketball in 1891, it was only six years later that a Yale University men's basketball team was credited with incorporating the use of dribbling in their team play. By 1909, full-on dribbling was allowed and practised more widely in the game.

58 BRICKLAYING

When you take a shot and completely miss the hoop or "shoot a brick," meaning the ball doesn't even remotely graze the hoop or the backboard, it's viewed as something incredibly bad that might have a profound psychological effect on the offending player who hurled up the shot.

For one, fans in the audience typically make fun of the player who shot the airball, screaming "airballllll" at the top of their lungs as a means to rattle them while they are running back on defence.

The perception of airballs has shifted over the last number of years, though, given the high volume of shots your average NBA player takes today versus yesteryear. Elite players like Los Angeles Lakers superstar Luka

Dončić or Milwaukee Bucks power forward/centre Giannis Antetokounmpo might take between twenty to twenty-five shots per game. Offensive superstars of yesteryear like Karl Malone or Charles Barkley took under twenty shots per game (Malone averaged 17.9 field goals attempted for his career, and Barkley averaged 14.5 field goals attempted per game).

So, who has been the greatest bricklayer in NBA history? Well, no one is certain. One of the reasons airballs aren't tracked by the NBA or by any college or professional leagues with the same statistical fervour as points, steals, rebounds, blocks, or assists, is that airballs do nothing to impact the actual outcome of any games.

Case in point: If you take a look at the trajectory of high-volume shooters like the late Los Angeles Lakers legend Kobe Bryant or perennial All-Star Carmelo Anthony, both of whom took a high volume of shots over their careers, they are often mentioned anecdotally as having shot a fair number of airballs, but that's only because they had a lot more opportunities to miss due to taking a lot more shots. It's all about the law of averages. And perspective is everything; if a player or team shoots above 50 percent, it would be considered a great game. And if a single player or an entire team is missing one-half of their shots, it means a sizable number of shots were missed in the broader scheme of things.

The biggest example of this airball discrepancy is if you watch a player like Steph Curry shoot an airball; it will have exactly zero impact on his decision to keep shooting. In fact, an airball may arguably even help sharpen the focus of elite shooters like two-time NBA champion Ray Allen, Indiana Pacers shooting guard Reggie Miller, or Curry, who will just come right back down the court and start draining a series of successful treys on their opponents!

59

GUNS AND ROSES

There is all kinds of NBA locker room urban folklore about teammates going at each other's throats in games and at practice, after a tough loss, or while competing for playing time. When the stakes are high, the adrenaline starts pumping, and players and teams are trying to strengthen their chemistry to get more wins than losses, anything is possible.

But on December 21, 2009, former NBA All-Star Gilbert Arenas took internal team tensions to a whole other level. Brandishing firearms in his Washington Wizards locker room because he had gotten into an argument with his teammate Javaris Crittenton over a gambling debt was downright moronic and scary. Arenas reportedly laid out four unloaded guns and told Crittenton to choose one.

Crittenton then allegedly pulled out his own loaded gun in response.

The incident led to both players receiving the stiffest penalty that the NBA has ever doled out for rule infractions: a suspension of forty-five games, or the remainder of the 2009–10 season. Arenas was also charged with a felony and sentenced to two years probation and thirty days in a halfway house. Arenas had always been known as a quirky, eccentric player who went by the nickname Agent Zero, but this incident effectively ruined his career. In the years following the incident, Arenas did express regret for his poor judgement: "I now recognize that what I did was a mistake and was wrong.... There's no such thing as joking around when it comes to guns — even if unloaded," Arenas said.

60

FOURTH QUARTERS

The NBA first caught a glimpse of the infinite earning potential of video games when *NBA Jam*, a two-on-two game created by Midway Games in the 1990s that featured some of the biggest stars in the NBA, including Michael Jordan, Hakeem Olajuwon, and Larry Bird, generated over one billion dollars in sales, in quarters.

Fast forward to today, and to say that the NBA video game market is lucrative would be an understatement. Consistently boasting annual sales in the millions (*NBA 2K1* sold over eight million copies in its first few months of commercial release), the NBA 2K franchise in particular is a cultural phenomenon that has captured the imaginations of hoop junkies and video game nerds alike since its inception in 1999. Published by 2K Sports and developed by Visual

Concepts, NBA 2K consistently secures the bag for the NBA, its investors, and distributors, and its ubiquitous social influence on basketball enthusiasts worldwide means that the NBA benefits enormously, marketing-wise, since the video game helps audiences both new and old engage the sport in ways that can't be measured in fiscal terms.

When *NBA Jam* hit the commercial marketplace in the 1990s, most video game fiends got their fix playing basketball digitally on coin-operated mobile units located in designated public arcades, bars, restaurants, and convenience stores. And that was just in its first year of operation. The fast-paced gameplay, multiplayer functions, and distinctive features (after making three baskets in a row, players can go into "on-fire mode" and gain extra turbo firepower and functionality) found in those early *NBA Jam* games left an indelible impact on even the most casual video game players and observers. Likewise, the distinct and catchy in-game commentary (like the announcer Krikow yelling "boomshakalaka!" after a great play was executed) and glitchy analogue audio soundtrack helped to further cement *NBA Jam*'s legacy as one of the most enduring arcade video games of all time, setting the stage for the dominance of the NBA 2K video game franchise of today.

61

THERE IS A COUNTRY FOR OLD MEN

When NBA and elite-level professional basketball players decide to hang their jerseys up in the rafters, the feeling has always been that there ain't no country for old men, or women, since the game has always been tied to youth.

With the average age of NBA players usually hovering around twenty-five, and very few making it to their late thirties or even forty in their career, where can retired players go to keep their juices flowing, get a check, and appease basketball-starved fanbases in arenas and on TV?

Certainly, the Big3 league, founded by rapper/actor Ice Cube and entertainment executive Jeff Kwatinetz, has helped fill a bit of that void. It's a unique three-on-three televised tournament, which diverges from traditional five-on-five full-court play. The league hires mostly retired NBA pros and gives them a chance to compete long after their careers have wrapped up. Says Ice Cube, "People think just because an athlete is not in the NBA, that he can't play at a high level. And we all know that's not true." With some NBA players segueing into coaching after their playing days are done, the league features unique player-coach jobs, where veterans like Chauncey Billups and Rashard Lewis have been given opportunities both to coach and play so that they can lead their teams both on and off the court.

For most retired players, it's either that or they leave America to go play in the slightly less competitive pro leagues in Europe or on the NBA Legends circuit managed by the National Basketball Retired Players Association, an arm's-length nonprofit supported by the NBA and the National Basketball Players Association with the aim of supporting retired basketball players with work opportunities long after their playing days are done.

62

DUMB JOCK

NBA players have to pay a "jock tax," income tax levied on athletes by different states and cities for the income they earn while playing in these locations.

The only things you are guaranteed in life are death, the distinct possibility that the modern-era Detroit Pistons might not make the playoffs with any consistency, and taxes. Regarding the latter part of this set of life's Unholy Trinity, NBA players have Michael Jordan to thank for portions of their lucrative contracts being handed over to Uncle Sam. The concept dates back to the early twentieth century, when states began to tax nonresident workers who earned income within their borders. However, it wasn't until the 1990s that the jock tax gained significant attention.

The modern jock tax can trace its roots to California's decision to tax the earnings of athletes from out-of-state teams when they played games in California. This move was reportedly motivated by Chicago Bulls star Jordan, who led his team to an NBA Championship victory over the Los Angeles Lakers in 1991. In response, Illinois enacted its own version of the jock tax, informally dubbed "Michael Jordan's Revenge," targeting California-based athletes playing in Illinois. Following California and Illinois, many states with major sports teams adopted similar taxes.

This rapid expansion led to a patchwork of state and local tax laws that athletes and their accountants had to navigate. The jock tax is typically calculated based on "duty days," which include the total number of days an athlete spends in a given state for games, practices, and other team-related activities. This tax means that NBA players, among other athletes, often file tax returns in multiple states each year. The compliance burden is significant, requiring meticulous tracking of days spent in various jurisdictions.

Critics argue that it unfairly targets high-earning athletes while ignoring other high-earning professionals who travel frequently for work. On Twitter/X, NBA champ Giannis Antetokounmpo half-jokingly mocked this taxation scheme showing up on his pay stubs, writing, "Who the hell is FICA and Jock can they hoop?"

The jock tax continues to be a significant financial consideration for professional athletes, influencing how they manage their income and taxes.

PS: Absolutely no one is feeling sorry for NBA players having to pay the jock tax, because despite these financial hiccups, the NBA is in a golden era of lucrative deals giving many players guaranteed multi-million-dollar contracts.

63
SENDA THE RECEIPTS

The erasure of the contribution of women from most things in society is like a plague. And basketball doesn't sit on a separate island.

While most basketball enthusiasts of all genders can rhyme off the tale of the father of basketball, Dr. James Naismith, who invented the game in 1892, if you mention the name Senda Berenson, you'll hear a pin drop. Despite Berenson's relative obscurity in the wider basketball court of public opinion, in reality her contributions loom large, since she began the women's basketball movement in 1893, just a year after Naismith invented the game.

As a physical education teacher and director at Smith College in Northampton, Massachusetts, Berenson essentially took Naismith's rules and adapted them for women, drafting up a whole new rulebook titled the *Basket Ball Guide for Women*. This was groundbreaking given that at the time women did not participate in team sports because it was thought by men at the time that basketball games would be too physical and rigorous for women.

By 1895, there were hundreds of women's basketball teams playing throughout the U.S., and Berenson even refereed the first women's basketball game at Smith College on March 22, 1893. This "Mother of Women's Basketball" deserves all of her posthumous flowers from the general public, much like the father of the sport.

64
DREAM AGAIN

For most amateur athletes, turning pro is the endgame. But what happens when that dream takes a detour? For Isaiah Austin, the 7'1" former Baylor University superstar, becoming a pro took on an entirely different meaning on June 21, 2014. It was on that day — a mere five days before the NBA draft — that Austin learned he had Marfan syndrome, a genetic disorder that weakens the body's connective tissue. Projected as a late first-round to early second-round pick, Austin had to take his doctor's advice and immediately halt his dreams of playing in the NBA, given that intense physical contact to his chest or sternum could potentially lead to death. It was also at this moment that Isaiah Austin became Isaiah Awesome, a dedicated Marfan syndrome activist.

Austin's coming out to the NBA brass about his condition a mere week before what was supposed to be a big day he dreamed about his whole life sent shivers down the spines of most hardcore basketball enthusiasts. And it was on June 26, 2014, immediately after the fifteenth pick of the 2014 NBA draft, that NBA Commissioner Adam Silver made Austin a ceremonial pick, without the promise of him ever playing basketball again. It was a classy gesture that the NBA has never done before in its history.

Austin operates his own foundation, the mission of which is "to inspire others to dream again." *Dream Again* is also the title of his 2015 autobiography. "We have to do the work out here to try to inspire as many people as we can while trying to raise awareness of Marfan Syndrome," Austin said at an NBA Cares event for All-Star Weekend. Despite the fact that one in five thousand people have Marfan syndrome, including men and women of all races and ethnic groups, according to the Marfan Foundation, if not for Austin's bold and public declaration of his diagnosis, the awareness of the disorder might not be as large as it is right now.

Outside of perhaps hearing that musician Bradford Cox (Deerhunter), Joey Ramone (Ramones), and Abraham Lincoln had Marfan syndrome, the disease does not get as much media attention and public support as, say, cancer and other more common illnesses. In his book, he recounts, among other things, that he had been secretly playing with blindness in his right eye due to an injury he sustained in middle school. "I haven't exactly had the easiest of times getting to where I'm at now," explains Austin, "but it's these bumps in the road that have made me a stronger person, a stronger man today." In the U.S., the Marfan Foundation, established in 1981, provides grants for research on Marfan syndrome and sponsors fundraising events to help raise awareness of the condition, which they write "often goes undiagnosed among health care providers and the public."

65

FOOTBALL × BASKETBALL =

Two of the fastest-growing and most popular sports in the world are soccer (football) and basketball. So, what would happen if you blended elements of both sports to create a new one? Well, that has already happened thanks to some Swiss physical education teachers, Michal Lato, Piero Quaceci, and Pascal Roserens, who in 2015 coordinated a summer sports camp, National Sports Camp Switzerland.

After observing that the physical coordination skills of the kids in their sports camps were lacking, they dreamt up this idea to create a sport and educational game for school kids and clubs called FooBaSKILL that involves players attempting to achieve some mastery over two opposing sports while playing on two opposing teams. Their bottom line was not necessarily focused on improving the athletic performance of campers, but rather to focus on the kids acquiring and improving their fine motor skills.

When playing FooBaSKILL, the rules of both basketball and soccer aren't manipulated, but rather, there is a flip-flop that occurs between both teams, which have four players each. In the first half of the game, one team tries to score on the basketball hoop in a traditional way, and then on the flip side this same team is tasked with defending against the opposing team scoring goals. By the time the second half rolls around, the teams switch sides and reverse their roles. The rationale behind pushing this sport is that both the upper and lower body are being worked out skill-wise, simultaneously, whereas when you play either sport individually, that's not exactly the case. The playing field features on one half of the pitch two soccer goals, whereas a basketball hoop lies on the other half of the pitch.

The latter half of the pitch consists of parts of a gymnastic box with a cone or the FooBaSKILL goal on top. Players also use the side and back walls to bounce the ball off as they are navigating the playing field. As of press time, we're still not exactly sure whether it would be more appropriate to yell "gooooaaaal" or "splash!" or both ("splash, gooooaaaal!") when points are scored.

66

A BASKETBALL-LESS BASKETBALL

Of course, it feels next to impossible to imagine the sport of basketball being played without an actual basketball, but at the 1904 Summer Olympics in St. Louis, Missouri, basketball was only included in the games as a demonstration sport, so the idea of America fielding a "Dream Team" or collection of the best basketball players in the country to compete against the world's best was not even on the radar.

In fact, while testing out the sport of basketball's feasibility to take part in the biggest global sporting event in the world, let's just say that the two opposing teams played in less than ideal conditions, outdoors on shaky, dirt-ridden courts.

Oh yeah, and, uhhh, the players also used a soccer ball in place of a basketball to shoot and score points. In the early 1900s, the sport was still in its nascent stage, and the equipment and rules had not been universally standardized, so these particular games featured many experimental elements. In fact, these early Olympic gaming processes made up a part of a larger athletic competition, the Louisiana Purchase Exposition, which demoed and exhibited different emerging sports to test out their viability for global sports-loving countries and communities. As to what was chanted by fans to celebrate someone scoring during these times (Gooooaaaal?), that is unknown.

67

LITHUANIA LOVES HOOPS

In Lithuania, basketball is the national sport, and it is treated like a religion. In fact, the sport's elevation in the small country of 2.69 million's cultural consciousness can be traced back to its separation and emancipation from the Soviet Union in 1990. The country became the first of the old Soviet republics to secede. And this strong and consistent nationalist fervour carried over to the basketball court, where the Lithuanian national basketball team has traditionally performed well on the international stage, winning a number of Olympic bronze medals, the first coming in 1992.

The 1992 team's success was immortalized in the documentary *The Other Dream Team*, which takes place at the first Olympiad after the break-up of the Soviet Union, when the national team included Lithuanian players playing in the NBA. This team had also received some financial backing from legendary rock band the Grateful Dead, who had heard of the team's plight and decided to chip in.

The Lithuanian national basketball team's bronze-medal-winning success on the world stage carried all the way over to the late 1990s (1996), the early 2000s (2000), and to the 2010s, in which they won a bronze medal at the 2010 FIBA World Cup. The team has also won multiple European championships, the last being in 2003.

Likewise, a solid crop of world-class Lithuanian basketball players has competed on some of the biggest stages and leagues in the world, including the NBA. From 7'3" centre Arvydas Sabonis, who blazed a trail playing for the Portland Trail Blazers and is widely regarded as one of the greatest European basketball players of all time, to Šarūnas Marčiulionis, another pioneer for Lithuanian basketball who plied his trade for the Golden State Warriors, to current NBA centre Jonas Valančiūnas, who has played for the Toronto Raptors, Memphis Grizzlies, New Orleans Pelicans, and Washington Wizards, to Domantas Sabonis, the son of Arvydas, who has made a name for himself in the NBA with the Indiana Pacers.

Within the country itself, small towns such as Prienai have been capturing international headlines for the most peculiar reasons. For example, in 2018, LaVar Ball, the father of NBA pros Lonzo and LaMelo, sent his highly recruited sons, nineteen-year-old LiAngelo and sixteen-year-old LaMelo, to Lithuania, of all places, to develop their skills playing for a local club, BC Prienai Vytautus, as a segue to playing in the NBA. In what might have arguably been one of the most bizarre moves by highly regarded American basketball players in the history of the sport, LaVar's Big Baller Brand aimed to rescue the club from impending bankruptcy in 2018 but in the end was alleged to have destroyed the club, or so claimed head coach Virginijus Šeškus in a press release.

"The first and most crucial mistake we made was allowing them, especially LaVar, think that they are in charge of the club — its decisions, its plans, and even the game. His boys where [sic] nowhere near the level of the LKL, let alone NBA, which the league obviously understands, seeing the draft outcome. And the most disappointing fact was that they had no inner drive to become better. And when they saw it was going nowhere, they started destroying the club, not paying out prize money to the Big Baller Brand tournament winners, etc.," explains Šeškus.

"After leaving the club without any prior notice and by taking back their financial support, including shooting machines that were presented as gifts to the club, BBB has left Prienai without sponsorship and base for future planning." He added, "It was a short-term move, and it did the job — the club survived, and that is the most important fact. This season we are also making bold moves, but now we look to the big picture and future. We will give priority to professionals with great discipline and personalities."

68

VOTED LEAST LIKELY TO TAKE AN L

You've probably heard or read about some of the longest regular-season win streaks in the NBA. There was that 1971–72 Los Angeles Lakers squad led by the indomitable Wilt Chamberlain, assist maestro Jerry West, and scoring wiz Gail Goodrich, which pulled off a string of thirty-three consecutive wins, including two back-to-back undefeated months of play. Or how about, in more recent times, the Steph Curry–led Golden State Warriors that carried a twenty-eight-game win streak over two seasons (2014–15, 2015–16), culminating in an NBA regular season record-breaking win-loss record of 73–9?

However, when it comes to consistent sky-high winning percentages carried out over decades, none of these legendary squads can hold a candle to the Harlem

Globetrotters, a touring exhibition basketball team founded in 1926 that owns the best winning percentage in the history of professional sports. Over nine decades, the team has only lost some three-hundred-plus games. And while the Globetrotters do play a theatrical, entertaining, and comedic style of basketball, and most of their games feel like exhibition games that aren't attached to any professional basketball league, their rosters of highly skilled players who can shoot, dribble, dish, block shots, and dunk with the best of them are no joke.

The roster has over the years included such NBA legends as Connie Hawkins, Wilt Chamberlain, and basketball icons like Olympic gold medallist Lynette Woodward, their first female signing in 1985. While the team primarily travels the world playing one team, the Washington Generals, they have played exhibition games against NBA, NCAA Division I, and national teams from various countries, including Brazil, Italy, and China.

69 TRIPLE DOUBLES

With the advent of positionless basketball, players are more now than ever expected to play and guard multiple positions instead of being pigeonholed into playing a single position like point guard, small forward, or centre. What this has also meant is that there has been a flurry of modern players who are able to seamlessly and simultaneously score, rebound, block shots, and drop dimes.

From NBA veteran Russell Westbrook, who recorded the most triple doubles (forty-two) in one season (2016–17), and the most of the modern era, once averaging thirty-two over a 123-game streak, to Los Angeles Lakers star Luka Dončić or Denver Nuggets NBA champion centre Nikola Jokić, they carry this innate on-court third eye or sixth sense that has turned them into triple-double machines.

In 1946, one hundred years before the advent of positionless basketball, Joe Fulks was the first player ever to score a triple-double in an NBA game, before "triple threat" status became a thing. Far ahead of his time, Fulks was a pioneering player whose versatility made him one of the earliest prolific scorers in professional basketball. In the league's inaugural 1946–47 season, he averaged 23.2 points per game, leading the BAA (Basketball Association of America), a precursor to the NBA, in scoring. Standing at 6'5", which was considered quite tall at the time, his athleticism and shooting innovation (he popularized the jump shot, a radical departure from players shooting hook shots and taking set shots) allowed him to utilize a rare court vision that Dončić fans applaud today. Fulks's Philadelphia Warriors were crowned BAA Champions in 1947. It came as no surprise to anyone that he would be inducted into the Naismith Memorial Basketball Hall of Fame in 1978.

70

GRIZZLIES GO BELLY-UP

To say that the NBA is a very lucrative business would be the understatement of the decade, since the league boasts a collective valuation of $115 billion in 2024 and signed a media rights deal with TNT/Amazon in 2024 that's worth $1.8 billion per year. As a business entity, the NBA rarely fails, boasting some of the fastest-growing revenue streams in all of pro sports. But every now and then, the league experiences some bumps in the road. And one of those big bumps was the Vancouver Grizzlies, a Canadian basketball franchise the league had set up that failed quite quickly and miserably.

The Grizzlies franchise was launched in 1995, and after only six years of operation, the league pulled the plug and relocated the franchise to Memphis in 2001.

So, what exactly happened? Was it their overvaluation and drafting at number six — in their first NBA Draft lottery — of Bryant "Big Country" Reeves, a large, sluggish, awkward centre from Montana who listened to country music and did not fit the mold of what an NBA player played and looked like back then? And was that one of the early signs that suggested that the franchise was not ready to compete in the modern-day NBA? Or was it when they selected elite guard Steve Francis out of the University of Maryland with the second overall pick in the 1999 NBA Draft Lottery, and then he publicly stated that he had no desire to play in Vancouver, Canada, of all places, a city with no real professional basketball pedigree or history to speak of? Was it just bad business decisions being made by the ownership group, Orca Bay Sports and Entertainment? Or was it all of the above and then some?

According to documentary filmmaker Kathleen Jayme, who has shot a few profound documentary films (*The Grizzlie Truth, Finding Big Country*) about the Vancouver Grizzlies franchise and one of its former marquee players, it wasn't any one of those phenomena that ultimately sank the franchise. "I don't think there was just one thing that led to the Grizzlies moving to Memphis. There isn't a specific person or team personnel to blame," says Jayme. "It was a series of unfortunate events — the expansion rules, two NBA lock-outs, low CAD dollar, young team, the list goes on and on…. The team could never quite catch a break! Despite this, fans showed up, and the love for the Grizzlies in Vancouver still remains strong today."

71

A PENNY FOR YOUR THOUGHTS

With NBA stars of today getting paid quite handsome salaries for their on-court endeavours (in 2024–25, megastars like Steph Curry, Joel Embiid, Nikola Jokić, and Kawhi Leonard each earned between $51.4 to $55.76 million in a single season), it gets increasingly difficult to believe or imagine that there was actually a time when NBA stars weren't paid so well and didn't even care to think about processing large banknotes.

For example, back in the mid-1970s, the inventive and splashy American Basketball Association, which eventually merged into the NBA, featured an eclectic and idiosyncratic player named Marvin "Bad News" Barnes. On the court, Barnes was a wizard with the basketball, dating back to his college days at Providence University between 1971 and

1974, where he averaged 20.7 points and 17.9 rebounds. At 6'8", Barnes was a prolific scorer and playmaker who would ultimately be drafted by the Philadelphia 76ers with the second overall pick.

However, it was when Barnes was not playing basketball within those ninety-four-foot lines that things would go astray, since he did heavy drugs and was arrested for gun possession, among other things. He later admitted to snorting cocaine during some games while sitting on the bench for the Boston Celtics. Nevertheless, at a time when pennies as a currency were in much larger circulation, Barnes refused to accept pennies as part of his salary disbursement or any of his financial transactions. He considered pennies to be an omen of bad luck. So he always requested to be paid in large increments. In 1976, he was fined $10,000 for missing team flights, and in true enigmatic Barnesian fashion, he paid the entire fine in pennies to drive home a point to the league that he should not be messed with.

72

THREE-POINT LAYUP

Will there come a point in time in basketball when knocking down a three-point shot is treated with the same level of difficulty as a simple layup? For example, in the NBA, three-point shooting numbers have skyrocketed since 2016 (the NCAA introduced the three-point line to college basketball in the 1986–87 season). In today's NBA, average teams shoot about twenty-five three-pointers a night. Should we blame it on Steph Curry, the greatest shooter of all time, who effectively turned three-pointers into layups? Or how about former Iowa Hawkeyes and WNBA All-Star Caitlin Clark, who shoots and hits three-pointers from otherworldly distances and locations on the court? We don't know who to blame, but what we do know is that a too-large bulk of middle school, high school, college, and pro basketball players have been jacking up shots from well beyond the thirty-foot line with no conscience since 2009, the year that Wardell Stephen Curry II was drafted into the NBA.

By all accounts, Steph is the greatest three-point shooter of all time, and it's not even arguable or open to debate. The late NBA champion Chris Ford, nicknamed "the Mad Bomber" for his affinity to shoot a truckload of threes, all the time, from everywhere, made the first three-pointer in NBA history, on October 12, 1979, so perhaps Steph has him to thank. It could be argued that Curry single-handedly turned three-point shooting into less of a role that a shooting specialist might occupy but more one that most players believe they should occupy. He has turned three-point shooting into being viewed as two-point shooting once was — and now many basketball laypersons genuinely believe they can and should hit three-pointers during pickup games, college basketball games, and in their own backyards.

And if you've seen Caitlin Clark play (arguably college basketball's greatest female player ever shoots threes from way beyond the arc), you'll see that hitting threes is meh and not that big of a deal nowadays. For good or ill, the game has turned itself into one big fat ninety-minute-long three-point shot.

73
ONE AND DONE

There's no sense denying it. When elite A-list high school basketball players make the decision to attend college in the United States, it's not with the intent to actually attend college and graduate. So this baked-in idea we have of university students taking full course loads over a four-year span to earn an undergraduate university degree is just not a realistic part of their master plan. Essentially, the only reason the vast majority of elite university basketball players attend college is because they have to, as part of an NBA Draft rule that states that high school basketball players can't go straight from high school to the NBA.

According to the current NBA Draft eligibility requirements, a player must be at least nineteen years old and be at least one year removed from their high school graduation. This rule, known as the "one-and-done" rule, was implemented in 2005 because the NBA and its teams wanted to ensure that players were more physically and mentally mature before entering the league. Additionally, spending time in college or playing in developmental leagues (including the G League Ignite team that the NBA set up in 2020 to accommodate this line of thinking, providing an alternative pathway to the traditional college route) allows players to gain more training, development, experience, and visibility.

There has been an ongoing debate about this rule, and some discussions suggest it could change in the future. But for now, basketball-playing college kids are not so much interested in hanging around college to earn credits; it's all about escaping college to go pro or exhausting one's name, image, likeness (NIL) earning potential. If not for the NBA rule, the vast majority of high-ranking five-star high school ballers would attempt to make the leap from high school straight to the pros.

And this is not an entirely new concept either. There was a time when high school players could skip the distraction known as college and head straight to the NBA Draft. Years before the one-and-done rule was legislated, all kinds of players attempted to make the leap, and more than a few were very successful (LeBron James, Kobe Bryant). And still a whole host of other players like prodigious 6'10" centre

Leon Smith, 6'7" small forward Korleone Young, and 6'11" small forward Jonathan Bender could have benefitted from playing college basketball because they were unable to meet the mental and physical demands of the NBA. Smith in particular became one of the poster boys of this failed idea, since he only ended up playing in fifteen total games and suffered severe mental health issues that required hospitalization.

Most who didn't make it became unspoken educational lesson plans on why basketball players with heavy-duty hoop dreams and no education need to have a backup plan if they don't make it to the league.

74
FOUR-POINT PLAYS

Between hitting three-point shots (see: Steph Curry, Caitlin Clark) and scoring your average everyday layups, dunks, and jump shots for two points, getting those bonus free-throw points for being fouled while scoring is a great way to add to a player and team's scoring totals.

In simple terms, if a player is fouled in the act of taking a two-point shot that they hit, they are awarded a free throw, and if they hit that shot, presto, that's three points. The same thing goes for shooting a three-pointer, hitting the shot, and being fouled in the act. If a player hits that bonus free throw, it's a quick and easy four points added to the player and team's scoring totals.

Make no mistake about it, four-point plays are quite rare. And there are two players in the history of the NBA who have achieved some mastery in repeating this rare feat. Jamal Crawford, the silky-smooth shooting guard who won Sixth Man of the Year award three times (2010, 2014, 2016) over his twenty-year career, once held the record for most four-point plays in NBA history. He was known for his ability to make a trey while drawing a foul.

In more recent years, former NBA MVP and ten-time All-Star James Harden, referred to as "the Beard," is known for his scoring (he was a three-time back-to-back-to-back scoring champion from 2017–20) and proficiency in converting four-point plays. Harden's process all begins with his dribbling mastery, with which he is effectively able to cross up defenders, and then you couple that with his ability and efficiency in taking step-back three-pointers. Consider this: For a six-year span (2014–20), Harden led the NBA in free-throw attempts. And according to Basketball Within Borders, since the NBA started tracking play-by-play stats in 1996–97, Harden had completed the most (ninety-five) as of 2024.

75
SHOT BLOCKERS

The NBA has employed some fantastic shot blockers over the years, with most of the league's top shot rejecters standing near or above seven feet tall.

For the likes of 6'11" NBA Hall of Fame centre Hakeem Olajuwon, who holds the record for the most blocks in NBA history (3,830), and 7'4" behemoth Mark Eaton, a two-time defensive player of the year whose primary role was to rebound and block shots, their blocks-per-game averages typically hovered between 3.1 to 3.5 respectively. Essentially, a great defensive player playing in any modern-era game who is able to average at least two blocks per game is a big deal.

In a game that had to have been seen to be believed, Sudanese-American Manute Bol, one of the greatest shot blockers in NBA history and one of the tallest players as well at 7 feet 7 inches, blocked eleven shots in a single half of a game. While playing for the Washington Bullets against the Atlanta Hawks on January 25, 1986, Bol's 7'7" wingspan played huge dividends in this regular season game that his team lost. Most NBA centres can't accumulate eleven blocks over the span of five or six games, never mind one half, so let's just say that his formidable presence in the post during this game firmly cemented his icon status in the BasketBol annals.

76

CHA-CHING/C.R.E.A.M.

One of the reasons basketball is one of the fastest-growing sports in the world is because it is also one of the best-paying sports in the world. And who in their right mind doesn't want to secure the bag?

In fact, basketball is the highest paid sport in the world, with an average annual salary in the NBA in 2023 of nearly $10.5 million. That is more than double the average salary in the NFL, which sits in second place at $4.5 million. And some of its most highly visible players, like LeBron James, may become members of the billionaires club.

Why do professional basketball players out of all of the other major sports get paid so handsomely? There are a plethora of reasons, but the NBA generates much more substantial revenue through ticket sales, merchandise, sponsorships, and broadcasting rights than the other leagues. The league's lucrative TV deals alone bring in billions of dollars, significantly boosting overall revenue. Basketball as a sport, and the NBA in particular, also enjoys immense global popularity, whereas a sport like NFL football is a lot more provincial and is more widely watched in North America than anywhere else.

The NBA's growing worldwide fanbase translates into higher merchandise sales, international broadcasting deals, and sponsorships, contributing to the league's financial success. The NBA also operates under a salary cap system, which sets a limit on how much teams can spend on player salaries. The cap is tied to league revenue, so as revenue increases, the salary cap rises, allowing for higher player salaries. The league's collective bargaining agreement (CBA) has played a major role in increasing salaries, since the National Basketball Players Association (NBPA) negotiates the CBA with the league, which then outlines salary structures, benefits, and revenue-sharing. The CBA ensures players receive a significant portion of the league's revenue, leading to higher salaries.

Lastly, NBA players versus, say, NHL or MLB players, are a lot more marketable and tapped into hip-hop and pop culture trends and are able to secure more lucrative endorsement deals as a result. This marketability enhances their overall earnings and raises their value to teams, also contributing to higher salaries.

77

CAREER SHORTS

When sports enthusiasts think of pro sports that have short career spans, they often reference full-contact sports like football due to its over-the-top physicality and higher than average injury rates. But NBA players typically have shorter career spans than those in many other professions, and as a result they receive higher than average salaries to compensate for the limited time they have to earn revenue at peak levels.

Despite basketball not being a full-contact sport, its average career span is quite low at four to five years, and there are many key factors cited. For example, you'll notice that NBA general managers have been drafting younger players over the years, including many one-and-dones from the college ranks. The thinking behind this is that players who enter the NBA at a younger age will have experienced less wear and tear on their bodies and thus have the potential for longer careers, given the eighty-two-game regular season schedule. Also, given the small size of typical NBA rosters, with teams able to have up to fifteen players and there only being thirty teams in the league, with up to 450 players maximum per year, there are just not a lot of jobs to go around.

If we look at a league like the NFL, the average team's roster usually carries about fifty-three players, and that's excluding an additional sixteen salaried players that teams can keep on their practice squad roster. So, despite the short average career span in football, which sits at, on average, three to four years due to its higher risk for injury and the more extreme physical demands, there are lots of jobs in that league, sometimes up to two thousand per year. Also, the steady influx of new talent from college and international players overseas annually presents a challenge for players for roster spots, which directly impacts the career longevity of your average NBA player. NBA teams can have up to two players on two-way contracts, allowing them to move between the NBA and their developmental G League, but that still comes nowhere close to an NFL football roster.

78
PAID PINSTRIPES

Being an NBA referee is arguably one of the lowest public profile positions in the league, after the players, coaches, general managers, and cheerleaders.

If you were to quiz your average basketball fan about who their favourite referees are and why, you might be met with silence. In fact, the only referees who seem to get any media attention are the ones who are chastised for making consistently bad calls or are linked to betting and point-shaving scandals, like Tim Donaghy, who went to prison for his gambling misdeeds. Despite all of that, and outside of media sightlines, NBA referees secure the bag at rates that few are aware of. NBA referees earn the highest salaries of any of the major pro sports leagues. While NFL referees have higher average salaries ($205K per year), their base salary peaks lower than the NBA's top earners, who can earn upwards of $500,000 annually, with significant bonuses added for officiating in the playoffs and finals.

Most NBA referees start out with an annual salary of $150,000, but the league's higher-end salaries trump those of NHL referees, for example, who cap out at $400K per year. The pay is well deserved, since the NBA's season is long, the fitness requirements are intense, given the fast pace of the game, the rules of the game are intricate, and the high-pressure stakes of having to endure intense scrutiny from players, coaches, fans, and the media are no joke.

79

BLACK HISTORY MONTH, YEAR, LIFE

You don't have to be a race relations expert to deduce that the NBA has the highest percentage of Black players of any of the major four professional sports leagues (NBA, NFL, MLB, NHL) in North America. All you have to do is watch any NBA game. In 2023, approximately 70.4 percent of NBA players were Black, with whites constituting the second highest racial group at 17.5 percent. The next highest reporting racial group was multiracial at 9.7 percent, with 2.2 percent identifying as Hispanic, and only 0.2 percent of players being of Asian descent. All of which makes the actual history of the league that much more intriguing in that when the original NBA was formed in 1949, it was an all-white league, and the roles were completely reversed. By the next year, the league had started to integrate and allowed the first African-American player, Chuck Cooper, to play. Cooper was drafted fourteenth by the Boston Celtics in the second round of the NBA Draft, and the pick was met with skepticism by some in the NBA, including some of the Celtics' owners. But Celtics founder and original owner Walter Brown famously said that Cooper could be "striped, plaid or polka dot … all I know is the kid can play basketball, and we want him on the Boston Celtics."

Cooper's selection provided a pathway for other Black players to play in the league. That same year, the New York Knicks signed Nat "Sweetwater" Clifton to a contract, the first significant contract signed by a Black player, and later that year, Earl Lloyd of the Washington Wizards became the first Black player to actually play in an NBA game. And since then, there's been no turning back.

80 NINE-ON-NINE, ANYONE?

Basketball was not always a five-on-five sport. By and large, when we think about the average basketball team's membership and roster, the composition of the squad should have five players whose role it is to try and fill out these distinct positions: point guard, shooting guard, small forward, power forward, and centre. In general terms, the point guard, who is the primary ball handler, has almost always been the smallest player on the floor, though that has been changing in recent times (see positionless basketball), and your tallest player, who is usually tasked with taking game-opening jump balls, blocking shots, and grabbing rebounds, is typically the centre.

When Dr. James Naismith invented the sport in 1891, the game was played with nine players on each team, since

Dr. Naismith divided up his physical education class of eighteen students into two groups to test the new game. And the original rules did not specify a set number of players, leading to varying team sizes in different regions and schools.

The first known basketball game with five players on each team took place on January 18, 1896, between the University of Iowa and the University of Chicago, and as the game spread and gained popularity, the five-on-five format began to be standardized. By the early 1900s, most teams had adopted the five-on-five format, and it became the norm due to its balance of allowing sufficient player movement and maintaining team dynamics, which were well suited to the size of most indoor courts. The five-on-five format was officially adopted by the key governing bodies of basketball like the Amateur Athletic Union, and it was codified in the rules of the game, making it the standard for competitive play at all levels, including high school, college, and professional leagues. Today, five-on-five is the universally accepted format for standard basketball games. However, other variations of the game, such as three-on-three, are also hugely popular and have their own rules and competitions; three-on-three was included for the first time at the 2020 Tokyo Olympic Games.

81

LATE BLOOMERS (THE JORDAN RULES)

When most young wannabe basketball players at either the middle or high school level are cut from the team after open tryouts, they usually take that as a sign to quit the sport and continue playing it for recreational and noncompetitive purposes or try their hand at another sport. And then others use these strong feelings of disappointment as fuel to train harder, come back stronger, and never let the word “cut” enter their vocabulary again.

The urban fable of Michael Jordan, widely considered the greatest basketball player of all time, getting cut from his high school basketball team during his sophomore year isn’t actually true, but it’s pretty close. What actually happened was that Jordan, who attended Emsley A. Laney High School in Wilmington, North Carolina, tried out for the varsity basketball team as a sophomore but did not make it. Instead, he was placed on the junior varsity (JV) team. Not making the varsity team as a sophomore fuelled Jordan's determination to improve. Training with his older brother James, who was only 5'7" and was considered a better player and dunker than him, he worked hard on his skills and quickly became a standout player on the JV team, often scoring forty points a game. By his junior year, Jordan had grown several inches and significantly improved his game, earning a spot on the varsity team. He went on to become a star and was heavily recruited by NCAA schools from across the U.S.

Jordan ultimately committed to the University of North Carolina and hit what ended up being the game-winning shot in his freshman year as his team won the 1982 NCAA championship against the Georgetown University Hoyas. Jordan himself has referenced that rocky high school tryout experience as being a pivotal moment in his career, motivating him to work harder and become the best.

82

RIM RAISING

The standard and universal height for a basketball hoop in junior high, high school, college, and pro leagues around the world is ten feet (3.05 metres), a measure that has been in place since the game's invention by Dr. James Naismith in 1891. But should basketball rims be raised taller than ten feet? Well, here's the reality. Human beings are getting taller. For example, the average height of American males during the late nineteenth century, when basketball was invented, was five feet six inches, whereas in 2024 the average height of adult males was five feet nine inches.

Back in the seventies and eighties, dunking a basketball used to feel like a superhuman act that was the provenance of taller and more athletic men. Today, dunking is quite pedestrian. It's also become too easy for taller players to dunk and score now, and we see this at all levels of play, from high school and college, all the way to the pros. Would taller hoops help reduce the frequency of dunks, encourage players to develop more versatile shooting and passing skills, and help level the playing field, thus reducing the advantage of exceptionally tall players and emphasizing athleticism, technique, and strategy? Perhaps. On the other hand, raising the height of the rim beyond its current ten feet would mean having to completely retool how the game is played, from shooting to rebounding. And that would also mean rewriting all of the NCAA, WNBA, and NBA records, statistics, and comparisons across eras that were based on players playing on a ten-foot rim.

The game has evolved in many other areas: adding a three-point line, expanding the key, changing the size and structure of the blackboard, and changing the style of rim, so it's curious that a movement to raise rims hasn't gained as much steam. Certainly, in the women's game there is absolutely no focus or attention paid to dunking the ball because so few women players can dunk on ten-foot rims, so the argument to raise basketball rims becomes even more moot.

83

SEVEN-FOOT UNICORNS

Basketball remains the only major professional sport where recruiting seven-foot-tall players, who are exceptionally rare in the general population, is an obsession for high school, college, and pro scouts, recruiters, and coaches. And there might come a time when eight-footers are on the horizon, given the ascent of players like 7'9" Canadian centre Olivier Rioux. Naturally, seven-footers carry innate advantages when it comes to scoring close to the ten-foot rim (such as by dunking), rebounding, altering, and blocking shots from the opponent. With the globalization of the game in full effect, the idea of North American scouts struggling to find and recruit rare seven-foot centres is dated, since seven-foot players are a dime a dozen now, especially outside of the West.

A steady herd of seven-footers have arrived in the NBA, with no signs of slowing down: 7'6" Yao Ming (China), 7'7" Gheorghe Muresan (Romania), 7'7" Manute Bol (Sudan), 7'3" Victor Wembanyama (France), 7'4" Zach Edey (Canada), 7'4" Boban Marjanović (Serbia), 7'6" Tacko Fall (Senegal), 7'4" Rik Smits (Netherlands), 7'2" Arvidas Sabonis (Lithuania), and 7'2" Kristaps Porziņģis (Latvia). It's true: The air up there is getting crowded.

84 PREGAME RITUALS

In most professional sports, players have pregame rituals that range from the mundane to the absurd, and NBA players are no exception.

Many basketball players not named Dennis Rodman are viewed as programmable and robotic, and it's easy to understand why, since successful pro athletes have to be able to adhere to team formulas and systems, execute predetermined plays drawn up by coaches, and toe the line, especially when it comes to rhyming off predictable generic soundbites at press conferences.

But the idiosyncrasies you may not see on the court and on the sidelines do come out in different ways. And watching the pregame rituals of some basketball players gives you a bird's-eye view and a strong glimpse into their actual personality type. A sizable number of NBA players are known for their unique, bizarre, and wildly interesting pregame rituals. NBA icon LeBron James carries out a chalk toss ritual before every game. He dips his hands into a bag of chalk powder, claps them together, and throws the chalk into the air, and no one knows why. But his ritual is tame compared with other players in the NBA fraternity, like 2011 NBA champion and combo guard Jason Terry, who would wear the shorts of the opposing team the night before games. Retired NBA small forward Caron Butler sometimes chewed on straws during games to comfort himself. Dynamic point guard Kyrie Irving burns sage and walks around smudging the court on game day to create positive energies inspired by his Native American heritage. And even four-time NBA champion Steph Curry does this thing where he sprints at full speed across the court after executing his hyper-detailed pregame ritual that involves a series of dribbling drills and shots, including long-distance shots from the players' tunnel, which help him get into rhythm.

85

YOU'RE (NOT) BEAUTIFUL, IT'S TRUE ... TO BE BLUNT

When fans arrive at college and professional arenas to take in live games, not only are they there to cheer on their home team or boo and hiss the opposing team, but they also enjoy taking in the ambience, energy, and aesthetic of the arena and its surroundings. It's what makes paying to see a high-profile college or NBA game a full-on fan experience that stimulates the senses and not just the pocketbook. And it makes fans want to come back for more. Good-looking arenas with well-designed basketball courts play into that experience. Case in point, the Los Angeles Clippers' splashy and aesthetically pleasing Intuit Dome, which opened in 2024 and features hi-tech double-sided halo boards complete with player and team statistics alongside gameplay videos and images.

While most college or pro basketball courts carry similar or mostly the same standard layouts that include free throw lines, three-point lines, the paint (key), and a centre circle used for the jump ball at the start of the game based on the team's internal design scheme, the colour codes and design templates that end up landing on the court craft a unique visual identity for branding purposes that can be either distinctly good or annoyingly bad.

For example, the 2024 NBA champion Boston Celtics play at the TD Garden, which is known for its distinctive parquet floor, while the Brooklyn Nets, who play at the Barclays Center in Brooklyn, are known industry-wide for their unique black-and-white floor colour scheme, emblematic of the team's colours. Some of the main considerations that go into the designs are the materials like wood, which is standard for professional courts, and the team colours, which influence the visibility and aesthetic appeal.

In the NCAA, arguably the most jarring court to look at for long stretches of time is the University of Oregon's court, the Matthew Knight Arena (named after the son of Nike founder Phil Knight), which features a loud forest design with pine trees around the perimeter, representing the state's natural beauty. The court's primary colours are shades of brown and green, further emphasizing the forest theme. The arena is one of the most talked-about basketball courts in the world, for all of the wrong reasons, because of its confusingly bright, bold, jarring, unconventional, and visually busy design elements.

86

JUST SAY NO

The use of recreational or performance-enhancing drugs before, during, and/or after sporting events has long been a sore spot for professional athletes, and basketball players do not sit on a separate island.

In the history of the NBA, thirty-five players have been suspended for drug use. There are numerous tales of players of yesteryear getting high before, during, and after games. David Thompson, a Hall of Famer, battled cocaine addiction during his career in the late 1970s and early 1980s. Len Bias, who was drafted second overall by the Boston Celtics in 1986, died of a cocaine overdose just days after the draft. Former NBA star guard Michael Ray Richardson's career with the New York Knicks and New Jersey Nets was plagued by drug addiction issues, and he was handed a rare lifetime ban in 1986 after repeated violations of the NBA's drug policy. Richardson was reinstated by the league a few years later, but he was a pale shade of his former self. And still others, like Dallas Mavericks centre Roy Tarpley, had their careers cut short due to repeated violations of the NBA drug policy.

One of the most notable tales of NBA players admitting to using drugs is former Los Angeles Laker and two-time NBA champion Lamar Odom. In his memoir, *Darkness to Light*, Odom revealed that he had used cocaine before games during his career, and his admissions shed light on the personal challenges he faced despite his success on the court.

The NBA's approach to drug use has certainly evolved over the years, based on some of these revelations by former players, coupled with research and literature that strongly suggests the league's policies were racially driven. In the 1980s, the league introduced random drug testing and a structured drug policy, which has been modified to address new challenges, including the use of performance-enhancing drugs and marijuana. In recent years, the NBA has softened its stance on marijuana use. As of 2020, the league and the players' union agreed to suspend random drug testing for marijuana, including delta-8 and CBD, reflecting shifting societal attitudes and the legalization of marijuana in several states.

87

EIGHT POINTS IN NO TIME (OR ELEVEN SECONDS)

If you're a legit three-point shooting threat, your likelihood of getting fouled while hurling up a three-pointer and then converting that into a four-point play increases. But what happens when you are able to convert two back-to-back four-point plays in quick succession? Sounds next to impossible, right? And if a player pulls that off, what was the defensive team thinking, if they were thinking at all? But that's exactly what happened when the Miami Heat's sharpshooter James Jones, the 2011 NBA Three Point Contest champ, hit two three-point shots in succession, getting fouled on both plays, and then converted both free-throw attempts. Impossible. But it happened.

And this Jones-fuelled scoring outburst against the Atlanta Hawks on April 29, 2009, all happened within an eleven-second span. The 6'8" three-point specialist and three-time NBA champion played on five different NBA teams over his career, and his job description was pretty clear as a hired gun: shoot threes.

88

TEXTBOOK TWEENER

In basketball, being labelled a "tweener," a player whose physical attributes and skill set don't fit perfectly into conventional roles, is tough.

Kenny Lofton Jr. is the textbook definition of a basketball tweener, largely stuck in pro basketball purgatory due to his size, not skill. At 6'6", he's too undersized to play his natural power forward position in the NBA, since he utilizes a wide array of scoring moves in the post or key, moves that players four inches taller are supposed to be pulling off. And weighing in at 275 pounds, he lacks the foot speed and athleticism to play the small forward or shooting guard positions that match his height. None of these metrics seemed to matter collegiately, since he starred for the Louisiana Tech Bulldogs and led Team

USA to a gold medal at the 2021 FIBA Under 19 World Cup in Latvia.

Lofton is also the only player in basketball history to hold the distinction of having scored more than fifty points in a G League game and more than forty points in an NBA game. A walking bucket and a prolific scorer in the paint, where he scores more than half of his buckets, one would think that by putting up these lofty Lofton-like stat lines, he would be a sure bet to have a secure NBA career. Well, not so fast. When Lofton scored forty-two points in an NBA game, his first, it was while playing for the Memphis Grizzlies in the season finale where they were already out of playoff contention (read: that's when deep bench players finally get some playing time; the game's result played zero role in how the Grizzlies' year ended). Essentially, the only reason Lofton Jr. has bounced around the league on short-term two-way NBA contracts with the Memphis Grizzlies, Philadelphia 76ers, and Utah Jazz is because he does textbook tweener things that traditional stats just can't and won't reveal.

89

FILIPINO FEVER

Basketball is the number-one sport in the Philippines, and that's not open to debate. Given that basketball is a sport largely dominated by players who are tall in height, and considering the average Filipino male stands at 5'4" (females at 4'10"), what's the connection? And why the fixation on basketball and not some other sport? Well, the sport arrived in the Philippines more than a hundred years ago as an import of U.S. colonial rule. And by 1911, the sport had become a part of the country's public school physical education curriculum. Also, one of the main turning points in the Filipino community's preoccupation with basketball can be traced back to 1954, when the national team won a bronze medal at the FIBA Basketball World Cup — the only time an Asian country has ever medalled at a global basketball event. This was an incredible result, given the very limited financial resources doled out by the government for the national team, formal training, and basketball skills development.

Historically, no home-grown Filipino player has made it to basketball's promised land, the NBA — even highly touted 7'3" prospect Kai Sotto, a.k.a. "the Filipino Unicorn," went undrafted in 2022 — and the few that have just happen to be biracial, such as 1978 NBA draftee Raymond Townsend, the first Filipino American player drafted, and Jalen Green, Jordan Clarkson, Dylan Harper, and Ron Harper Jr. That hasn't slowed down this vibrant country of 116 million people's obsession with the game. And the NBA has reciprocated some of that love, hosting Filipino Heritage Night in more than a dozen NBA franchises, dating back to the first one hosted in 2008 at the Golden State Warriors' home court at Oracle Arena.

Off the court, the Filipino basketball cultural revolution officially took off and took shape when legendary NBA coach Pat Riley announced Erik Spoelstra as the new coach of the Miami Heat in 2008. It was significant in ways far outside the actual score of the games or the team's win-loss record in that Spoelstra became the first person of Filipino descent to be a head coach in the NBA, and in any of the major North American sports leagues. He has since gone on to win two NBA championships while coaching two of the greatest players of all time, LeBron James and Dwayne Wade.

And home-grown Filipino basketball legends like Jimmy Alapag, a 5'9" former wunderkind guard, are following in his footsteps. Alapag was hired in 2023 as the Sacramento Kings' player development coach and back home in the Philippines is renowned for his stellar national team play as a floor leader running the point guard position from 2007–13 and for accumulating a long list of accolades that includes six Philippine Basketball Association championships and one season MVP. Alapag was a mainstay for the Philippine national team, earning the nickname "the Captain."

90

GOING RIGHT AND LEFT

In a basketball strategist and coach's mind, finding a major weakness in an opponent's game almost always centres around identifying their dominant dribbling and shot-making hand, right or left. And then you base your defence around the weaker hand as a means to exploit this supposed weakness. This strategy almost always works at the high school, college, and even pro levels, since players usually have a preferred dominant hand with which they like to execute plays. But what happens when a player is ambidextrous and can "take you" (drive, finish) with either hand, and you can't necessarily force them to go right or go left to exploit their weaker hand?

Interestingly, there are a number of NBA players who are ambidextrous, which makes it not so easy to put together strategies for opposing defences. For example, NBA champion point guard Kyrie Irving is naturally right-handed but can shoot with his left hand with equal ease. Australian small forward and NBA pro Ben Simmons shoots with his left hand, despite being right-handed. Others, like Mike Conley or WNBA legend Candace Parker, are all technically right-handed but tend to shoot left-handed with equal ease and efficiency. And then others, like LeBron James, a right-handed shooter, eats and signs autographs with his left hand.

"Are they going left or right" is the question, to which there is sometimes no answer.

91
BALLS AND NETS

There are some highly competitive sports played around the world that are very basketball-esque, and it's surprising that they get very little attention in major world media and popular culture.

For example, netball, a limited-contact team sport in which two teams of seven try to score points against one another by shooting a ball into a high hoop that closely resembles a basketball hoop, remains primarily popular in Commonwealth countries such as Australia, New Zealand, and the U.K., as well as various parts of Africa and the Caribbean. The sport has yet to cross over in any significant way because the sport is largely played by expatriates of the aforementioned Commonwealth countries. Netball was formerly played exclusively by women but today features mixed-gender competitions, and the ANZ Championship was quite popular in Australia and New Zealand as the premier netball league before folding up shop in 2016. But despite the sport's basic similarity to basketball, it just hasn't been able to generate broad-based sponsorship deals and media coverage, severely limiting its visibility and financial growth.

92
DUNK CUBED

The common basketball act of throwing down a dunk is singular, as in, it is typically only one basketball that is being thrown down into a hoop with authority. That all changed at the 2011 NBA-All Star game Sprite Slam Dunk contest, when 7'0" centre JaVale McGee did the unthinkable and pluralized the act by dunking three balls in a single jump.

McGee ended up losing in the final round of the juried dunk contest to Blake Griffin, a decision basketball fans question to this day given the much higher degree of difficulty of the dunks he pulled off throughout the contest. But the consolation prize for this heightened aerial creativity as he jumped with two balls in his possession and then dunked each prior to receiving and slamming an alley-oop pass (from then-teammate John Wall) was landing in the *Guinness Book of World Records* for the Most Basketballs Dunked in a Single Jump.

93

FOR US, BY US, ABOUT US

Historically Black colleges and universities (HBCUs) have been underrepresented in elite-level college basketball recruiting circles, and they do not have the reputation of being pipelines to get players drafted to the NBA. In fact, the last HBCU player to be drafted in the first round of the NBA draft was Tennessee State University forward/centre Carlos Rogers in 1994. So, in 2020, when highly ranked Kenyan-Australian player Makur Maker, a 7'0" centre/power forward and cousin of then NBA and Australian pro players Thon and Matur, decided to turn down scholarship offers from top Power 5 college-to-NBA incubator schools like Kentucky and UCLA, it sent shockwaves throughout the NCAA and the NBA. For HBCUs, it created a great recruiting and unpaid marketing ripple effect whereby top Black high school recruits started seriously considering attending an HBCU for the unique Black cultural experience they would receive, something that could not be found attending a predominantly white school.

ESPN broadcast superstar Stephen A. Smith, himself an HBCU graduate and college basketball player at Winston Salem State University, had this to say about Maker's move: "When you are Black and you are in a predominantly white environment, you find yourself feeling isolated and alone.... Suddenly, you go to an environment and you're surrounded by people who look like you, that share your cultural background, and that go through some of the same trials and tribulations as you go through. Therefore, you're not alone.... You're pushed, you're motivated, and more importantly, you're supported.... I'm very proud of [Maker]. I'm grateful for him making the decision that he made.... We all win in this."

While Makur ended up being the highest-ranked five-star prospect to attend an HBCU, ranking as high as number 12 on high school recruits by 247Sports, his time at Howard University was cut short and marred by injuries and the Covid-19 pandemic, which limited his ability to play a full season.

94

QUADRUPLE DOUBLE

It's fair to say that most elite basketball players have achieved mastery over at least one or a few of the skills, like scoring or rebounding, needed to succeed at the pro level. Well-rounded basketball players that have mastered multiple skills simultaneously are able fill out the stat sheet in any of the four trackable categories: points, rebounds, assists, and blocks.

Basketball culture rewards players who are able to record a "double double" (which tips the hat to players who achieve any combination of two of the aforementioned trackable stats in double figures) or a "triple double" (which records any combination of three of the aforementioned trackable stats in double figures). Since the WNBA's inception in 1997, only a small group of players have achieved this feat, with legend Sheryl Swoopes recording the first triple double on July 27, 1999, as a member of the Houston Comets, finishing with fourteen points, fifteen rebounds, and ten assists. Fast-forward to 2024, when the Indiana Fever's Caitlin Clark became the first WNBA rookie to record a triple double with nineteen points, twelve rebounds, and thirteen assists in an 83–78 win over the New York Liberty.

But what about achieving a quadruple double, which means racking up double-digit stats in all four areas, points, rebounds, assists, and blocks? Well, it almost never happens, and in the history of the NBA or the WNBA, only a remarkably tiny list of players (four) has achieved this rare stat line. It's never happened in the history of the WNBA, and in the over hundred-year history of the NBA, only Nate Thurmond, Alvin Robertson, Hakeem Olajuwon, and David Robinson have produced a quadruple double. Finding players whose game contains this virtual Swiss-army knife toolkit of basketball skills is incredibly rare.

95

DENNIS THE MENACE

It'd be too easy to brand NBA legend Dennis Rodman a partied out, multi-tattooed, one-trick pony who just rebounded the ball well and did little else to help his teams win. Certainly, after winning five NBA championships and playing a key role on the two teams (Detroit Pistons, Chicago Bulls) that he won them with, the only thing that you can brand him as is a winner. That being said, Rodman's rebound-dominant and eerily lopsided career stats (he only averaged 7.3 points per game and 1.8 assists per game against a 13.1 rebounds per game clip) point to a guy who took great pride in being somewhat one-dimensional and a player who aimed to achieve complete and utter mastery and dominance over this one skill: rebounding.

Simply put, over the last forty years in the NBA, Rodman is the only player ever to have recorded almost four dozen (forty-six) games played where they scored no points despite having played more than thirty minutes per game. The next player closest to that, at thirty-two games, is another largely one-dimensional rebounding maestro, Ben Wallace, who had an even lower points-per-game average than Dennis (5.7) but wasn't nearly as dominant and focused on cleaning up the glass as Rodman.

If Rodman's rebounding numbers and consistency don't speak to his commitment to mastering the art of rebounding with at times reckless abandon, and his accompanying passion for life, then we don't know what will. Rodman grabbed rebounds and went after loose balls like his life depended on it. And in his NBA Hall of Fame speech, it really *did* feel like his life depended on it. "I didn't play the game for the money, I didn't play the game to be famous," he told the audience before describing his life circumstance of being abandoned at the age of five by a father who had forty-seven kids in the Philippines. "This game's been good to me. You know, I could have been anywhere in the world. I could have been dead. I could have been a drug dealer. I could have been homeless.... I *was* homeless."

96

MICKEY D's GOES GLOBAL

The annual McDonald's All-American All-Star Game features the *crème de la crème* of elite high school basketball players and has been a great predictor of future success.

Beginning in 1977 as a boys-only showcase and then expanding to include girls in 2002, the prestigious game boasts a lengthy list of alumni who have gone on to have Hall of Fame–worthy careers, including Magic Johnson, Michael Jordan, Candace Parker, Kobe Bryant, LeBron James, A'ja Wilson, and Kyrie Irving. Despite its "All-American" name, and all of the games being played in America, given the globalization of the game of basketball, all kinds of international players have been chosen to participate in this prestigious event.

The first international player to play in the McDonald's All-American Game was 7'0" Canadian centre Bill Wennington in 1981. Wennington went on to have a successful pro career, winning three NBA championships from 1996–98 with the Chicago Bulls. In subsequent years, international players from countries like Canada would start to infiltrate the All-American game rosters as kids from around the world relocated to America to play for highly regarded prep schools as a means to fast-track their process into the NBA. Given the steady rise of talents coming from Canada since the early aughts, the game is now known as a showcase of North American talents, with elite-level Toronto high school players, from Olu Famutimi, the first Canadian player ever chosen to play in the game, in 2003 (he had to sit the game out due to injury), to NBA veterans Tristan Thompson and Cory Joseph, who played in 2010, or Andrew Wiggins (2013) and RJ Barrett (2018). In recent years, on the women's side, many elite Canadian players like Syla Swords (2023), Toby Fournier (2024), and Agot Makeer (2025) have played in the game and left their mark.

97

SHOOTERS SHOOT

The idea of taking shots from half court or full court has become relegated to kitschy contests in which fans can get a once-in-a-lifetime opportunity to win large amounts of cash if they hit the shot. But in professional basketball games, fans do get to witness thrilling half-court buzzer-beaters every so often.

Statistics for players hitting half-court shots are not officially tracked by the NBA, but we suspect that Steph Curry might hold that title, since he's hit numerous three-pointers near half court throughout his career. Curry also attempts and hits these shots during his warmup. Retired two-time NBA All-Star point guard Baron Davis hit the longest regulation shot in basketball history, on February 17, 2001, while playing for the Charlotte Hornets, when he heaved the basketball from beyond three-quarters of the court (eighty-nine feet from the basket) in a game against the Milwaukee Bucks. Davis had never in his career attempted a shot like this, and the longest long-distance shot he had ever made was thirty-one feet.

98

THE BLACK GODFATHER

The birthplace of basketball, Springfield, Massachusetts, where the game was invented and where the Naismith Basketball Hall of Fame is located, is quite well known. Likewise, many basketball enthusiasts can rhyme off who the "father" of basketball is, Dr. James Naismith. What's not known nearly enough is the story of the "birthplace of Black basketball" and its "father," despite the disproportionate number of Black players in NBA and NCAA college ranks.

As basketball was in its infancy in the early 1900s, a historically Black college and university (HBCU) graduate from Howard University, Edwin Henderson, also earned a phys. ed. Ph.D. at Central Chiropractic College in Kansas City, Missouri. While attending Harvard University in

1904 during the summer months and taking an athletic training class, he learned the finer points of basketball. He took this knowledge back to Washington, D.C., where he started teaching basketball at the local schools and at the 12th Street YMCA as the director of physical education for all of the Black schools in Washington. He then spent much of the rest of his life spreading the word about this beautiful game and subsequently became known as the "Father of Black Basketball." Henderson organized the Interscholastic Athletic Association, which assembled Black teams to play games along the mid-Atlantic coast, while some of the first HBCUs to adopt basketball were Hampton University, Lincoln University of Pennsylvania, Wilberforce University, and Virginia Union (Richmond).

99 MULTIGENERATIONAL CHIPS

While it's no secret that Tim Duncan is one of the greatest NBA players of all time, winning five NBA titles, two league MVP awards, and redefining the role of the cerebral big man, it's his elite consistency and longevity that really helps to define his contribution to the game.

While most players who win their first championship get major accolades and then are content to get older and collect large cheques through their contracts, Duncan seemed to get stronger as his playing days wore on. Having been a key contributor to one San Antonio Spurs NBA championship team in the 1990s (1999), three in the early 2000s (2003, 2005, 2007), and one in the 2010s (2014), Duncan is the only starter in the history of the NBA to win titles in three different decades. Nicknamed "the Big Fundamental" due to his mastery of the basic fundamental basketball skills (shooting, rebounding, passing, blocking shots), Duncan proved over a nineteen-year career that playing the game "the right way" is arguably more important than playing for highlights and that winning championships trumps hype, hoopla, and executing fancy dunks any day (read: his game had long been considered boring and not the most exciting thing to watch). In typical humble Duncan-ese, when asked near the tail end of his career in 2015 what had allowed him to be so good for so long, he replied, "A lot of luck, honestly. Same coach. Same organization. And just lucky to stay healthy."

100 THE SPOILS

Basketball pretty much formally became far less about fun and games when in 2021 the NCAA allowed players to earn as much revenue as they could while competing in American college sports under name, image, likeness (NIL) legislation, whereas in years past both scholarship and nonscholarship athletes were barred from getting paid to play because they were still considered amateurs.

But at a time when NCAA schools rake in hundreds of millions of dollars on the backs of their players, and head coaches also receive salaries in the millions (the University of Kansas head coach, Bill Self, was paid $9.6 million in 2023–24), the NIL rules allow student-athletes to generate revenues from their personal brand based on the Supreme Court's NCAA vs. Alston decision in 2021.

Within the big business of basketball today, the separation between church and state, and high schoolers and NBA players, is dissipating at a fast rate. The Amateur Athletic Union (AAU) circuit, where high school kids play for free to get their name out there to hopefully secure college scholarships, has increasingly become connected with the ambitions and business plans of multi-million-dollar NBA players looking to get these future legions of pros connected to sneaker company sponsors and the big bucks that may await them once they turn pro.

In 2024, NBA players sponsored — or operated — 37 percent of the elite, shoe-company-sponsored AAU clubs on the premier American travel circuits. This (still-growing) number speaks to the professionalization of America's developmental pipeline. The days of the "mom-and-pop" travel teams are long gone, replaced by big brands and household names.

"America's youth basketball industrial complex — fuelled by the financial incentives that drive the AAU basketball machine — has professionalized every level of American basketball," says film director Mike Nicoll, whose documentary *The Spoils: Selling the Future of American Basketball* perfectly breaks down the business behind the business of basketball. "The boundaries between AAU, NCAA, and NBA basketball are dissolving, and the truth is the business has now become the game."

101
THE FUTURE IS HER

NBA ratings and viewership continue to plummet, down 48 percent from 2012 to 2024 due to a laundry list of reasons such as NBA stars taking too many load management days off and too much three-point shooting. The exact opposite has happened in women's basketball: The WNBA has experienced record viewership numbers (the 2024 regular season was the most watched in league history), and for very good reasons, reflecting the league's growing popularity and increased interest in women's basketball.

With the WNBA expanding to include three new franchises in 2025 and 2026 (Toronto Tempo, Golden State Valkyries, and a Portland team), and with a whopping four of the twenty-five athletes chosen and ranked across all sports in *Bleacher Report*'s 2025 "Predicting the 25 Best Athletes of the Next 25 Years" being women basketball players (with Caitlin Clark at 2, Juju Watkins at 14, Paige Bueckers at 16, and Angel Reese at 23), there's no turning back on this ascent.

It certainly wasn't always like this. The league faced challenges in generating larger viewerships and widespread recognition due to all kinds of factors: gender bias (lack of support for women's basketball in general has always led to lower league investment and audience engagement), scheduling (the WNBA season overlaps with the NFL and NBA, competing for limited audiences), and lack of media coverage (in the late 1990s and early 2000s the WNBA received far less coverage than male-dominated leagues like the NBA), among other things. But led by WNBA superstars like A'ja Wilson, Breanna Stewart, Sabrina Ionescu, Angel Reese, Napheesa Collier, and Caitlin Clark, the league has been able to garner a lot more interest due to the sky-high level and consistent quality of play, and those ripple effects have been felt everywhere. NCAA women's games now typically rival the intensity of many prematurely elevated and celebrated men's games.

The WNBA has captured and capitalized on what the NBA once had: compelling narratives and storylines. The on-the-court competitiveness and racial chasm that exists between Angel Reese and Caitlin Clark has carried over from their college basketball battles, when Reese won a NCAA championship in 2023 as a member of the LSU Tigers, defeating the record-setting Naismith national player of the year Caitlin Clark's Iowa Hawkeyes. Certainly, the Caitlin Clark effect has helped to boost the women's game in unprecedented ways, coupled with the sheer skill and wizardry of players like A'ja Wilson, whose unmatched two-way dominance led to 2022 and 2023 WNBA championships for the Las Vegas Aces, multiple All-WNBA first team selections, and a WNBA record-tying fifty-three-point scoring effort in 2023 (she shares the record with Liz Cambage).

ABOUT THE AUTHOR

Photo by Stephen Bambo

Dalton Higgins is a publicist, educator, journalist, and author who has written six books centred around pop culture, including *Much Master T: One VJ's Journey*, *Hip Hop*, *Hip Hop World*, *Fatherhood 4.0*, *Far From Over: The Music & Life of Drake*, and *Rap N' Roll: Pop Culture, Darkly Stated*. Once long-time media pro Higgins learned to throw down a two-handed vertical dunk with ease in high school at the undersized height of 5'11", his obsession with basketball took hold. Over the last three decades, Higgins has interviewed a long list of NBA legends, including the late great Moses Malone, Allen Iverson, and Patrick Ewing; covered his hometown Toronto Raptors; reported on numerous NBA All-Star Games, beginning with Michael Jordan's last All-Star Game in Atlanta; and has worked with the NBA's Read to Achieve program. Higgins has managed PR campaigns for a wide range of film and TV broadcast properties, including the high school basketball CBC TV series *Anyone's Game*, centred around the hugely successful high school basketball program at Orangeville Prep that produced NBA champions Jamal Murray, Oshae Brissett, and Luguentz Dort. One of his favourite journalistic moments was penning a cover story on back-to-back NBA MVP Steve Nash. A walking, talking encyclopedia of hoop knowledge, Higgins's b-ball fanaticism continues unabated.